Reforming education and changing schools

Case studies in policy sociology

Richard Bowe and Stephen J. Ball
with Anne Gold

ROUTLEDGE

London and New York

First published 1992
by Routledge
11 New Fetter Lane, London EC4P 4EE

Simultaneously published in the USA and Canada
by Routledge
a division of Routledge, Chapman and Hall, Inc.
29 West 35th Street, New York, NY 10001

© 1992 Richard Bowe, Stephen J. Ball and Anne Gold

Typeset in Palatino by LaserScript Limited, Mitcham, Surrey
Printed and bound in Great Britain by
Mackays of Chatham PLC, Chatham, Kent

A catalogue reference for this title is available from the British Library

ISBN 0–415–07789–3
       0–415–07790–7

Library of Congress Cataloging in Publication Data
has been applied for

ISBN 0–415–07789–3
       0–415–07790–7

Reforming education and changing schools

The Education Reform Act introduced in England and Wales in 1988 is bringing about enormous changes in schools, both in management and as educational terms. This book is the first to look at the effects of the Act in all its aspects on the basis of empirical evidence gathered from schools over the first three years of the Act's implementation. It concentrates on three major aspects of change arising from the ERA: the local management of schools, the National Curriculum (particularly Maths, Science and English) and special educational needs. These are areas which have hitherto been treated in isolation by researchers. In fact, as each develops it has ramifications in other areas. Bowe, Ball and Gold preserve a sense of the complexity of this change process, and use their detailed research on the effects of the education reform act to examine more generally the processes of the implementation of reform and the management of change in schools. Throughout, their concern is with the *effects* of policy rather than with the *implementation* of the Act in any simple sense. Indeed they show that to regard policy as a fixed text is a fallacy. Instead it is a constantly changing series of texts whose expression and interpretation vary according to the context in which they are being put into practice.

This provocatively written and subtly argued book will be essential reading not only for all who want to know about educational reform in Britain, but also for anyone interested in the processes of educational change.

Richard Bowe is Research Fellow and **Stephen J. Ball** is Professor of Education at King's College, London. **Anne Gold** is a lecturer in the Management Development Unit of the Institute of Education, University of London.

Contents

Figures

Abbreviations

CPS	Centre for Policy Studies
DES	Department of Education and Science
ERA	Education Reform Act 1988
ESG	Educational Support Grant
GASP	Graded Assesment in Science Project
GCSE	General Certificate of Secondary Education
GERBIL	Great Education Reform Bill
HMI	Her Majesty's Inspectorate
HOD	Head of department
INSET	In-Service Education and Training
LEA	Local education authority
LFM	Local financial management
LMS	Local Management of Schools
MSC	Manpower Services Commission
NC	National Curriculum
NCC	National Curriculum Council
SAT	Standard Attainment Tasks
SEAC	Secondary Examinations and Assessment Council
SEN	Special Educational Needs
SMC	Senior Management Committee
SMP	Schools Mathematics Project
TVEI	Technical and Vocational Education Initiative

Preface

The research reported here was funded by the Strategic Research Fund of King's College London. We are most grateful to the Research Committee for their support. We also wish to acknowledge the excellent support we received from Liz Cawdron who transcribed all the interviews with great care, speed and accuracy. There are a number of colleagues at the Centre for Educational Studies at King's who also gave help, support and advice to the project; they include Margaret Brown, Arthur Lucas, Paul Black, Carrie Paechter, Meg Maguire, Alan Cribb, Robin Murray, Alister Jones and Shirley Simon. Geoff Whitty, David Halpin, Mike Wallace, Joe Blase, Tony Knight, Roger Dale, Brian Davies, Lawrie Angus and the MA students at Monash University, the MA in Urban Education students at King's and St Hilda's and BERA Conference participants also provided useful comment and support for our work. It is also important to underline our gratitude to the four schools with which we have worked. Every person we approached went out of their way to help with the research, and we much appreciate their candour, their time and their interest. We were pleased to find that several of those teachers who were most closely involved in the research felt that the research process had been useful and constructive for them as they confronted and coped with different aspects of the Education Reform Act.

Several pieces of the text have appeared in other places in other forms. The National Curriculum material in the *Journal of Curriculum Studies*, the LMS material in the BERA Dialogues series, the SEN material in a collection of papers edited by Roger Slee, an early draft of the management material was presented to a meeting of the ERA Research Network.

provisions of the Act.) We are also concerned with the ways in which change is being achieved. The ERA requires a whole variety of substantive changes; it also brings into being new ways of bringing about change. The case studies reported here are of two kinds. The primary data are drawn from case study research in four secondary comprehensive schools and two LEAs (although little of the LEA data are reported here). These also provide the basis for the second sort of case study; a focus upon two specific but major aspects of the ERA as it relates to schools – the National Curriculum (NC) and the Local Management of Schools (LMS). Our concern here is not to judge or evaluate the schools we studied, rather we aim to analyse and evaluate the *policies* and the impact of those policies. The book is about the 'effects' of policy rather than with policy 'implementation' in any simple sense. Indeed we are uncomfortable with the political and epistemological assumptions of 'implementation' research and attempt to establish an alternative, rival framework for our analysis of change (in Chapter 1). As you read this book some of the requirements and ramifications of these policies will still be in train. Thus, our account and our analyses cannot be definitive or final. This is a 'first look' at the ERA in practice and some of its effects, there will be many other views appearing in the coming months and years. But we would reject any argument which suggested that the data reported here merely identify some teething troubles or transitional difficulties. It is our contention that many of the problems and conflicts that we present here are inherent in the ERA itself. They will not go away. They derive from incoherence, contradictions and inconsistencies within the ERA policies themselves – 'the quality and practicality of the change project' (Fullan 1991, p.72). As Fullan goes on to say: 'Ambitious projects are nearly always politically driven. As a result the time line between the initiation decision and startup is typically too short to attend to matters of quality' (p.72). Unfortunately, both politicians and many researchers and commentators ignore this and take a narrow view and assume that any problems arising from change are indications of the weaknesses or resistance of those burdened with the tasks of changing. This is convenient but it is also sloppy and misguided. However, as we shall see, it is not unusual to find schools struggling to come to grips with multiple, disparate and incoherent reforms and blaming themselves for 'not getting things right'. We are not suggesting that schools never make mistakes and neither are we trying to defend some kind of golden age of education which the ERA is destroying. Indeed there are significant elements of good-will towards some aspects of reform in the schools studied (as well as grave suspicion about other aspects). But we do contend that there are political expectations and ideological projects embedded in the ERA which are destructive of values and relationships which are fundamental to the 'qualified universalism' of the 1944 Act and which impose on schools 'drudgeries and demands' which both undermine and divert from their ability and capacity to cope. In important respects the ERA fails to pass 'the test of the "practicality ethic" of teachers' (Doyle and Ponder 1977–78). Fullan argues: 'Good change is hard work; on the other hand, engaging in a bad change or avoiding needed changes may be even harder on us' (1991, p.73). We also argue that some of the intended and unintended consequences of the ERA policies actually have deleterious effects on educational provision and 'standards'. And that while some students and parents may truly benefit from these policies others certainly lose out.

The school and LEA case studies reported here were begun in the spring of 1989 and in a slightly different form are still continuing. All of the schools were LMS pilots in 1989–90 and took on the full responsibilities of LMS in April 1990. All the extracts from data quoted in the text are dated so that they can be located back into the change process. Data collection in the schools concentrated on senior teachers and school governors and those teachers (and advisers) involved in introducing National Curriculum mathematics, science, English and technology (we are grateful for Robin Murray's help with interviewing technology teachers) as well as those teachers involved in Special Educational Needs work in two of the schools (this was Anne Gold's main responsibility) and some teacher 'bystanders' who we asked to comment on the general process and effects of change in their school. Several department heads and senior teachers were interviewed on more than one occasion, some on several occasions. This provides a sense of change over time and allows us to comment on the dynamics, the pace and the increasing complexity of change (Chapter 6). In the LEAs we interviewed directors, subject advisers and inspectors, and LMS officers. In all 90 interviews were recorded. In addition some governors' meetings were observed, as well as some senior management team meetings, some in-service activities and some department meetings. We aimed to get to know the schools well. We were given free access to all staff, meetings and to the documents we requested, although the degree of our involvement is uneven across the four schools. This is because we became particularly interested in particular things at certain points in time. The research strategy was regularly reviewed and like good ethnographers we tried to feed analysis back into data collection. Interviews and observations were analysed by coding and constant comparison (Strauss 1987).

The two LEAs in the study are referred to as Westway and Riverway. Both are small; Westway has 14 secondary schools, Riverway eight and a tertiary college. Westway is controlled by a Labour council and Riverway by a Liberal Democrat council. The two case-study schools in Westway – Flightpath and Parkside – are mixed 11–18 comprehensives. The Riverway schools are both 11–16, Overbury is mixed and Pankhurst is single-sex girls, it is the only single sex school in the LEA. The headteachers of Flightpath and Parkside are male, those of Overbury and Pankhurst female.

The chapters in this volume can be read as a set of interrelated essays. Each chapter has a different focus but Chapter 1 provides a conceptual basis for the whole analysis. The range of data employed in each chapter varies; the management, National Curriculum and market chapters (Chapters 6, 4 and 2) use material from all four schools, the LMS chapter (Chapter 3) concentrates on one school and the SEN chapter (Chapter 5) on two. We were unable to present all the themes and issues to arise from the data nor can we present all the data relevant to those which are covered. But we do err on the side of more data rather than less. This is because of the complexity of the issues and the immediacy which can be conveyed by direct speech. We have tried to avoid major overlaps but there are some points where bits of data or points of analysis are repeated. This we think is inevitable because of the interrelated and inter-affecting nature of the policies examined. LMS has implications for the curriculum, management is closely related to the market, SEN decisions have implications for the budget etc., etc. Thus, in a way, this should not be read as a neat, single narrative, it is rather a set of overlaid and overlapping analyses. The themes in each chapter are one set of cuts through the data, and ways of seeing the ERA. To reiterate, the themes are not exhaustive.

If we can anticipate and underline two messages that emerge strongly in our data and therefore in our commentary and analysis (and there are several others) they are; first the immense complexity of the changes facing schools in the wake of the Education Reform Act of 1988; and second, what is being lost or jeopardized by these changes – trust, commitment, co-operation and common purpose.

Chapter 1

The policy process and the processes of policy

INTRODUCTION

In the field of educational policy studies the 'placing' of schools, teachers and students in the policy process, has been largely achieved by theoretical fiat. On the one hand there has been extensive work on the generation of policy. This has remained, for the most part, within the province of macro-based theoretical analyses of policy documents and the activities and organization of groups of policy makers. Concern here has been with the representation or exclusion of interests in the political process and the struggles of activists, pressure groups and social classes within that arena (Kogan 1975, Ball 1990a). In these conceptualizations schools remain either marginal to the policy process or they are 'represented' via the teaching unions. The voices of the heads, senior managers, classroom teachers or the students remain, for the most part, strangely silent. On the other hand, there has been a growing body of literature investigating the 'implementation' of policy. This has often taken the form of detailed analyses (micro-based ethnographies for example) of how the 'intentions' behind policy texts become embedded in schooling or, more frequently, of how aspects of the schooling situation 'reflect' wider developments in the political and economic arena. There has also been a somewhat smaller body of literature that has celebrated the potential power of teachers and/or students to subvert the heavy hands of the economy or the State. Here the silent voices are heard, but they speak either as theoretically overdetermined mouthpieces of a world beyond their control or as potentially free and autonomous resisters or subverters of the status quo.

This separation between investigations of the *generation* and the *implementation* of policy, has tended to reinforce the 'managerial perspective' on the policy process, in the sense that the two are seen as distinctive and separate 'moments'; generation followed by implementation (Alford and Friedland 1988). This distortion produces accounts of the policy process as linear in form; whether top-down, bottom-up or allowing for a 'relative autonomy' of the bottom from the top. Thus, state control theories (Dale 1989) portray policy generation as remote and detached from implementation. Policy then 'gets done' to people by a chain of implementors whose roles are clearly defined by legislation. In policy studies generally this sort of 'linear' conception of policy has been further encouraged, post-1979, by what has been increasingly referred to as the Thatcher 'style' of government and its avowed intention to break down the corporatism of the 'social democratic' consensus (CCCS 1981). The lack of wide consultation prior to legislation on the trade unions, the health service and in education was seen as evidence of a new, non-corporatist style in action. Thus, for example, Lawton has talked of the pulling apart of the old 'partnership' between the DES (Department of Education and Science), the LEAs (local education authorities) and the teachers and its substitution by a fragmented policy process in which the new policy makers appear remote from the educational scene; a scene which, nonetheless, the policy makers are trying to control more tightly (Lawton 1984). Thus, he considers the politicos (ministers, political advisers, etc.), the bureaucrats (DES officials) and the professionals, HMI (Her Majesty's Inspectorate) to have become increasingly 'disconnected' from the policy receivers (LEAs, schools and teachers) (Lawton 1984). If we take this 'tightening grip' (Lawton 1984) thesis further then the shift appears to have been taking place for some time. The growth of centrally administered policies, TVEI (the Technical and Vocational Education Initiative) run by the MSC (Manpower Services Commission, later to become the Training Agency), ESGs (Educational Support Grants) run by the DES, both on a 'bid and deliver' basis, would be examples of the State's growing control of education. The culmination being the Educational Reform Act 1988 with its centrally 'determined' policy prescription that gives the DES and the Secretary of State extensive new powers to direct the work of LEAs and schools. In this analysis the changing language of the policy process would be illustrative of deeper structural changes in the relationship of the State to educational institutions. Thus from the TVEI and ESGs, which introduced the 'delivery' of educational change, external 'monitoring', 'management' and 'evaluation' (Dale *et al.* 1990), we go through to NCC (National Curriculum Council) documents which pick up that language and also talk about the 'implementation by headteachers . . . of the National Curriculum', 'absorption by individual teachers of the National Curriculum', 'delivery of his or her (student's) entitlement' etc., etc. (See for example, *National Curriculum: From Policy to Practice*, DES, 1989a.)

There seems little doubt that there has been a State control element in the Government's approach to policy construction and a strong desire to exclude practitioners (or their 'representatives', the trade unions) (see Ball 1990a). Furthermore, we would accept that in the legislation the Government's promotion of parents and the market over the claims of the 'educational lobby', and its language of 'implementation' are all attempts to continue to exclude certain voices from the policy process. Nonetheless we want to suggest that it would be politically naive and analytically suspect to begin from the assumption that it has been possible to make that exclusion total; either in terms of policy generation or in terms of implementation. The example of TVEI is itself particularly telling in this respect.

POLICY ANALYSIS AND THE STATE-CONTROL MODEL

As a policy externally imposed upon schools TVEI was initially seen as a classic example of a 'top-down' model of curriculum reform, however, the actual experiences of researchers and teachers told a somewhat different tale. TVEI reached the statute books as an initiative of Margaret Thatcher, Lord Young and Sir Keith Joseph. It was well financed and required schools and LEAs to submit projects for scrutiny prior to finance being made available. Yet many have pointed out that the MSC's need to secure the co-operation of the 'educational lobby' actually produced curriculum development in schools that was far closer to the educationalist (mostly school-based) than the occupationalist (mostly MSC-based) model of the curriculum (Dale *et al.* 1990). The point is that the transformations that may come about as legislative texts are recontextualized may, in some cases, be dramatic. McCulloch (1986) argues, for example, that the utilitarian rhetoric and objectives that accompanied the launching of the initiative have been *subverted* via their incorporation into mainstream education. Although TVEI was successfully established in the context of Thatcherite politics at the national level, at the local level it gave way to a revival of more liberal notions of educational practice (Gleeson 1989 pp.88–9). Saunders (1985), referring to TVEI, has suggested three broad categories to indicate how schools generally responded to this externally initiated change:

1. Adaptive extension: A strong interpretation of TVEI – it has been used to change the whole curriculum.
2. Accommodation: TVEI adapted to fit the general shape of the existing curriculum structure.
3. Containment: TVEI absorbed by the existing school pattern.

While there are many problems with a static and uniform categorization of this kind (schools may shift position over time and different departments may respond differently and financial and staffing constraints may inhibit response) it nonetheless serves to underline the ways in which detailed curricular planning and implementation may be driven by different interpretations of change. In reading the literature on TVEI one is struck by the extent to which an externally 'imposed' policy was appropriated by the teaching profession for very different purposes to those intended by the policy. The implication is that the 'capacity' of the State to reach into the schools has to be judged via the use practitioners make of policy initiatives and, consequently, the extent of state control resulting from the 1988 Act actually remains an empirical question. Indeed we would go further and agree with West's observation about *Learning to Labour* (Willis 1977) and extend it to the sociology of education more generally:

> There is a relative lack of serious examination of institutional or organization mediations between capital and the classrooms experienced by the lads. Although other CCCS work does begin to address such issues of educational policy, professional alliances, etc., we still have little idea of how such national policy issues and processes connect to schools and classrooms, and how the latter connect to such groups as the lads.
>
> (West, 1983)

Thus, despite the very real sense in which teachers have been excluded from the 'production' of the Reform Act 1988, we still want to argue that a State control model distorts the policy process. Indeed it seems to us that the image implicit in the conception of distinct and disconnected sets of policy makers and policy implementors actually serves the powerful ideological purpose of reinforcing a linear conception of policy in which theory and practice are separate and the former is privileged. The language of 'implementation' strongly implies that there is, within policy, an unequivocal governmental position that will filter down through the quasi-state bodies (presently the NCC and the subject working parties) and into the schools. (The LEAs are placed in a marginal position, but are essentially seen to be supporting schools in their endeavours.) It is clearly in the Government's interest to promote such a view. Consequently, this top-down, linear model is hardly the best starting point for research into the practical effects of the ERA. *Who* becomes involved in the policy process and *how* they become involved is a product of a combination of administratively based procedures, historical precedence and political manoeuvring, implicating the State, the State bureaucracy and continual political struggles over access to the policy process; it is not *simply* a matter of implementors following a fixed policy text and 'putting the Act into practice'. One key task for policy analysis is to grasp the significance of the policy as a text, or series of texts, for the different contexts in which they are used.

POLICY RESEARCH AND THE ANALYSIS OF POLICY TEXTS

The translation of educational policy into legislation produces a key text (the Act). This, in turn, becomes a 'working document' for politicians, teachers, the unions and the bodies charged with responsibility for 'implementing' the legislation. Although questions about the status and the nature of particular policy texts remain empirical ones, we have found the work of Roland Barthes a useful, conceptual starting point here. He has argued that:

> literature may be divided into that which gives the reader a
> role, a function, a contribution to make, and that which renders

the reader idle or redundant, 'left with no more than the poor freedom to accept or reject the text' and which thereby reduces him to that apt but impotent symbol of the bourgeois world, an inert consumer to the author's role as producer.

(Hawkes 1977, p.113)

This latter sort of text he refers to as 'readerly', and the signifier/ signified relationship is clear and inescapable; there is the minimum of opportunity for creative interpretation by the reader. An initial reading of National Curriculum texts, for example, and their technical language of levels, attainment targets, standardized attainment testing and programmes of study, might suggest just such a readerliness. However, the NCC has also published secondary texts, the Non-Statutory Guidelines, which suggest the National Curriculum texts are to be interpreted more like Barthes alternative 'writerly' texts, which self-consciously invite the reader to 'join-in', to co-operate and co-author. In the language of TVEI, to feel a sense of 'ownership'. But this free play is a matter of degree in the interpretation and reading of these texts rather than any kind of open freedom of action. Barthes has also argued that: 'writerly texts require us to look at the nature of language itself, not through it at a preordained "real world"' (Hawkes 1977, p.118).

We have been acutely aware that the very invention of a new proposed 'reality' for schooling in terms of attainment targets, etc. draws attention to the language itself, and to its adequacy as a way of thinking about and organizing the way pupils learn. 'Making sense' of new texts leads people into a process of trying to 'translate' and make familiar the language and the attendant embedded logics. In this process they place what they know against the new. Readerly texts, however, presuppose and depend upon presumptions of innocence, upon the belief that the reader will have little to offer by way of an alternative. Teachers may feel battered and coerced, they may have been softened up for change, but they are also suspicious and cynical and professionally committed in ways that hardly form the basis for 'innocence'. Finally, Barthes suggests that the reading of writerly texts involves two kinds of 'pleasure', the straightforward pleasure of reading and the *jouissance*, the ecstasy or bliss which arise from the sense of breakdown or interruption. The latter coming from the critical and creative response to the text, the seeing through to something beyond. While this might produce for some a sense of discomfort and loss, it also opens up possibilities for 'gaps' and 'moments' of progressive and radical insertion, for example the breakdown of transmission teaching, subject boundaries and formal examining and their replacement with cross-curricular work, investigations and group and process-based assessments. What it is also vital to recognize then is that these readerly and writerly texts are the products of a policy process, a process that we have already indicated emerges from and continually interacts with a variety of interrelated contexts. Consequently texts have clear relationships with the particular contexts in which they are used. This applies as much to national debates as to exchanges in schools between teachers and the individual approaches developed by teachers to meet the requirements of the National Curriculum.

In looking at the 1988 Act a number of authors have already pointed out, it is not a text that is capable of only one interpretation and the various elements that make up the Act (the National Curriculum, LMS, Open Enrolment, Opting Out, etc.) empower different bodies, groups and individuals in different ways (Bash and Coulby 1989, Jones 1989 and Whitty 1989), empowerment depending not only upon the 'tightness' or otherwise of the legislation but also upon the possibilities and the limits of particular contexts and settings. In effect the ERA is being constantly rewritten as different kinds of 'official' texts and utterances are produced by key actors or agencies of government – Programmes of Study, Attainment Targets, Subject Working Party Reports, NCC Reports, etc., etc. Thus a whole variety and criss-cross of meanings and interpretations are put into circulation. Clearly these textual meanings influence and constrain 'implementors' but their own concerns and contextual constraints generate other meanings and interpretations. Thus while textual analysis:

> Makes it possible to understand knowledge production as a chain or series of transformative activities which range from the social organization of text industries, to the activities of text producers, through the symbolic transformations of the text itself, and to the transformative interaction between text and reader, or school knowledge and student.
>
> (Wexler 1982, p.286)

As Wexler goes on to point out, it is crucial that such analysis is critically informed by a political and social analysis that seeks to uncover some of the processes whereby such texts are generated. Texts, structures and agencies of control need to be attended to. The state control model actually tends to freeze policy texts and exclude the contextual slippages that occur throughout the policy cycle. Instead we would want to approach legislation as but one aspect of a *continual* process in which the locii of power are constantly shifting as the various resources implicit and explicit in texts are recontextualized and employed in the struggle to maintain or change views of schooling.

This leads us to approach policy as a discourse, constituted of possibilities and impossibilities, tied to knowledge on the one hand (the analysis of problems and identification of remedies and goals) and practice on the other (specification of methods for achieving goals and implementation). We see it as a set of claims about how the world should and might be, a matter of the 'authoritative allocation of values'. Policies are thus the operational statements of values, statements of 'prescriptive intent' (Kogan 1975, p.55). They are also, as we conceive it, essentially contested in and between the arenas of formation and 'implementation'. While the construction of the policy text may well involve different parties and processes to the 'implementing' process, the opportunity for re-forming and re-interpreting the text mean policy formation does not end with the legislative 'moment'; 'for any text a plurality of readers must necessarily produce a plurality of readings' (Codd 1988, p.239).

In our ethnographically-based study of policy our concern has been to explore policy-making, in terms of the processes of value dispute and material influence which underlie and invest the formation of policy discourses, as well as to portray and analyse the processes of active interpretation and meaning-making which relate policy texts to practice. In part this involves the identification of resistance, accommodation, subterfuge and conformity within and between arenas of practice and the plotting of clashes and mismatches between contending discourses at work in these arenas, e.g. professionalism vs. conformity, autonomy vs. constraint, specification vs. latitude, the managerial vs. the educational. Furthermore it is important to acknowledge that policy intentions may contain ambiguities, contradictions and omissions that provide particular opportunities for parties to the 'implementation' process, what we might term 'space' for manoeuvre (Wallace 1990). We want, briefly, to illustrate this approach by looking at the National Curriculum.

THE NATIONAL CURRICULUM AS TEXT AND THE POLITICAL CONTEXT

In a very real sense generation and implementation are continuous features of the policy process, with generation of policy (or recreation, Knip and Van der Vegt 1991) still taking place after the legislation has been effected; both within the central state and within the LEAs and the schools. What is more these different contexts of policy recreation are connected directly by their varying capacities to affect the work of each other. In our research on the ERA we have been constantly aware of the extent to which people in schools and LEAs discuss the alternative 'readings' of the broader political picture and the pronouncements of politicians, the policy 'implementing' bodies such as the NCC and SEAC (Secondary Examinations and Assessment Council) and the officials of the DES. These discussions provided varying interpretations of what 'they' (the legislators and the 'implementing bodies') wanted and varying views of what possibilities or limits these might create for the LEAs or the schools.

> Well when the first document came out, about '87, the red book I think, people immediately saw that as a very much back-to-basics, back to single subject definitions, especially percentages of each one. But now that the programmes of study are beginning to evolve, or at least the attainment targets and so on have shown they're not, and attainment targets emphasize cross-curricular links, people are moving now away from this subject definition again, towards the concept of cross-co-operation, and cross-curricular links and in fact I'm quite hopeful that the National Curriculum will be a stimulus for curriculum development, not a hindrance for it.
>
> (Deputy Head, Flightpath, 6 March 1990)

Thus the National Curriculum text enters into, as a new element, the *bricolage* of teaching, the cobbling together of bits and pieces into a 'pedagogic discourse' (Bernstein 1985). As a text it is decontextualized from its original location and then recontextualized into a new assemblage. The pedagogic discourse so constructed consists of 'the rules regulating the production, distribution, reproduction, inter-relation and change of what counts as legitimate pedagogic texts' (Atkinson 1985, p.171). In the generation and 'implementation' of policy the nature of policy contexts (classrooms, departments, schools, LEAs, NCC, SEAC, DES, 'think tanks', working parties, etc., etc.) and the relations between them become crucial to our understanding of how texts operate; although we must also remain aware of the ways in which texts change contexts and the relations between contexts. As Shilling points out, education policy is a dialectical process; 'policy outcomes are reliant upon the cooperation of the state, and an array of non-state organizations and individuals' (Shilling 1988, p.11), and importantly, in the case of TVEI, he argues that the outcomes: 'are constrained not only by the potential power schools are able to exercise as "front-line" organizations (Shilling 1986), but by fiscal and other institutional constraints (Offe 1985, p.306)' (Shilling 1988, p.11) (see Chapter 3).

Texts carry with them both possibilities and constraints, contradictions and spaces. The reality of policy in practice depends upon the compromises and accommodations to these in particular settings. Thus our conception of policy has to be set against the idea that policy is something that is simply done to people; although we accept that particular policy texts will differ in their degree of explicit recognition of the active (rather than passive) relationship between intended, actual and policy-in-use. One example is to be found in the recent statements, related to the National Curriculum, that are giving particular emphasis to the active participation of teachers. In various quarters teachers are being encouraged to 'make the National Curriculum their own'. There is an interesting and difficult double paradox in this in terms of education policy and politics. On the one hand the ERA and the NC are the outcome of a now typical process of macho, Thatcherite policy-making which rides roughshod over the interests and sensibilities of the teachers. In addition, years of strident critique from Government has sapped public confidence in, and the morale of, teachers. On the other hand, the implementation of the NC relies heavily upon the goodwill, commitment and energy of teachers. They must make it work. Since the Act came on to the statute books a number of senior Tory politicians have been engaged in a propaganda exercise to 'talk-up' teachers and praise their efforts and talents. Kenneth Baker, then

Secretary of State for Education, in the 1989 inaugural IBM Education Lecture at the Royal Society, asserted: 'I doubt that any country starts with a better or more effective teacher force than we have in Britain. Our teachers stand comparison anywhere in professionalism, dedication and imagination.' He then went on to say: 'The achievement in schools in the last three years in bringing in the new GCSE examination to a successful introduction is witness to that. The professional work now going on in schools all over the country to prepare the way for introducing the national curriculum inspires confidence that that too will be a job well done' (TES 1989). And the then Prime Minister herself, in a widely reported interview with the *Sunday Telegraph* on 15 April 1990, stated:

> Going on to the other things in the curriculum, when we first started on this, I do not think I ever thought they would do the syllabus in such detail as they are doing now. Because I believe there are thousands of teachers who are teaching extremely well. And I always felt that when we had done the core curriculum, the core syllabus, there must always be scope for each teacher to use her own methods, her own experience, the things which she has learned and he or she really knows how to teach.

A report of this was headlined in the following Friday's *Times Educational Supplement*, 'Mrs. Thatcher signals "U-turn" on curriculum'. In the article the reporters suggested the Prime Minister was concerned about the National Curriculum becoming too prescriptive. What was remarkable was her frequently repeated reference to the teaching force,

> So I did not really feel that the core curriculum or any subject should take up all the time devoted to that subject, because otherwise you are going to lose the enthusiasm and the devotion and all of the extras that a really good teacher can give out of her own experience.
>
> (TES 1990)

The point is of course, as Shilling notes, that the State must rely upon teachers to 'deliver' the curriculum. Consequently, to sustain a singular, National Curriculum requires either teacher acceptance and understanding, 'lock, stock and barrel' or a system for effectively policing teachers. A question of either 'winning the hearts and minds' of the workers at the chalkface – 'The commitment of individual teachers will be crucial in "making it happen"' (DES 1989, Secn. 9.14) – or creating the means whereby the State has the capacity to control and discipline the workforce specifically and directly. While there are clearly many elements of the latter embedded in the ERA, with 'implementation' at the forefront of governmental concern it is now strategically necessary, or perhaps inevitable, that proactive readings of the NC text be encouraged (what might be described as developing a degree of tolerance without fostering a sense of latitude). Thus, Duncan Graham, Chairman of the NCC until the summer of 1991, has said that, 'getting the National Curriculum off the ground will involve the talents of universities, colleges, LEAs and schools', and added, referring to the NCC itself, 'we have a highly professional Council which covers the main interests in the education service, with two exceptions all educationalists, people with practical hard-line experience of education, and it's turning out to have a gratifying mind of its own' (Talk at King's College, 18 January 1989).

However, the dilemma, tolerance without latitude, which the NCC as an organization represents and embodies, is never far from the surface. In the same talk Duncan Graham spoke of teachers as 'far more worried about their own position than the children passing through'. Teachers cannot be but must be trusted. This dilemma is increasingly evident in the official and semi-official texts which 'speak' the National Curriculum to schools. The recontextualization of policy in this case takes place in two stages, from Government, to agencies of sub-government (HMI, NCC, in-service and initial teacher education) and thence to the arenas of practice. The openness/closeness of text and the reactivity/proactivity of readings is a problem in both transitions. Thus the politics surrounding the work of the Subject Working Groups and the contradictory pressures on the NCC, alongside the emergent compromises in the ERA (Ball 1990a, Whitty 1989) mean the work of the DES and the NCC has two very different audiences. On one side there are the hawkish factions in the Conservative Party, on the other side are the teachers and the educational establishment. The first group must remain convinced that the National Curriculum will discipline teachers, raise standards and not pander to 'entrenched orthodoxies' (CPS 1988, p.6). The second must be reassured that the

National Curriculum will not become a vehicle for the 'loony Right' and will achieve a level of educational respectability. There have already been difficulties on both sides particularly in relation to the constitution and work of the NC Subject Working Parties. The Right have been disappointed with the work of the Science, Mathematics and English Groups (and the Kingman Report 1988) and the permanent members of the educational establishment are severely disgruntled with the reports of the English, Geography and History Working Parties. As regards the former, the Centre for Policy Studies have offered their own alternative *Correct Core* and comment:

> The CPS Core Curriculum sets out curricula for English, Maths and Science. In order to ensure that pupils leave school literate, numerate and with a modicum of scientific knowledge, it should not extend beyond these three core subjects, nor attempt more than set minimum standards in basic knowledge and technique.
> It is regrettable that these aims appear recently to have been abandoned by those in charge of producing and implementing education policy. As the following pages show, the official committees, the DES and Her Majesty's Inspectorate no longer adhere to the belief that teachers should teach and pupils should learn a simple body of knowledge and a simple set of techniques.
>
> (CPS 1988, p.59)

This perhaps serves to underline our view that policy, as knowledge and practices, as a discourse, is contested. It also points up the significance of influence in and control over critical sites of text production and recontextualization in the policy process. In this case the Subject Working Parties themselves and the NCC are prime examples of such crucial sites. To an extent the New Right have found themselves excluded until recently and thus limited in the effect they might have upon the production of 'official discourse' in these arenas. (They are, however, influential elsewhere in the whole policy process in education and they have gained some representation in SEAC, most recently with the replacement of the SEAC chair, Philip Halsey, by former No. 10 Policy Unit Head, Brian (Lord) Griffiths and also on the NCC, following the resignation of Duncan Graham, with the appointment of David Pascall, member of Margaret Thatcher's policy unit in the mid-1980s.) Consequently, even with a highly detailed piece of legislation on the statute books, educational policy *is still being generated and implemented both within and around the educational system* in ways that have intended and unintended consequences for both education and its surrounding social milieu. As a result the ERA and its attendant texts are in one respect an expression of sets of political 'intentions' and a political resource for continuing national debates, and in another a micro-political resource for teachers, LEAs and parents to interpret, re-interpret and apply to their particular social contexts.

CHARACTERIZING THE POLICY PROCESS

We want to end this chapter by indicating how we might move away *analytically* from a State control model, while still recognizing that the State, LEAs and schools are differentially empowered, over time, within the policy process. By introducing the notion of a continuous policy cycle we have tried to draw attention towards the work of policy recontextualization that goes on in the schools. However, researching the school setting actually requires us to consider not only the National Curriculum but also how the various elements that make up the ERA, LMS, Open Enrolment, opting out, etc., empower different bodies, groups and individuals in different ways. An heuristic representation of the policy process is represented in Figure 1.1. (This is the development of an earlier formulation in which, reading from the top and anti-clockwise, the contexts were labelled intended, actual and policy-in-use. We have broken away from this formulation because the language introduced a rigidity we did not want to imply, e.g. there are many competing intentions that struggle for influence, not only one 'intention' and 'actual' seemed to us to signal a frozen text, quite the opposite to how we wanted to characterize this aspect of the policy process.)

We envisage three primary policy contexts, each context consisting of a number of arenas of action, some public, some private (see Fig. 1.1). The first context, the *context of influence*, is where public policy is normally initiated. It is here that policy discourses are constructed. It is here that interested parties struggle to influence the definition and social purposes of education, what it means to be educated. The private arenas of influence are based upon social networks in and around the political parties, in and

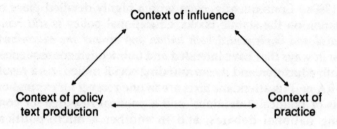

Figure 1.1 Contexts of policy making

around Government and in and around the legislative process. Here key policy concepts are established (e.g. market forces, National Curriculum, opting out, budgetary devolution), they acquire currency and credence and provide a discourse and lexicon for policy initiation. This kind of discourse forming is sometimes given support, sometimes challenged by wider claims to influence in the public arenas of action, particularly in and through the mass media. In addition there are a set of more formal public arenas; committees, national bodies, representative groups which can be sites for the articulation of influence. Clearly in trying to understand the education policy-making of the last three Conservative Governments it is important to be aware of the considerable 'capture' of influence by the New Right think tanks that operate in and around the Conservative Party (see Ball 1990a, Knight 1990). But it is also vital to appreciate the ebb and flow in the fortunes of and the changes in personnel of the DES, and to recognize the increasing 'ministerialization' of policy initiation (see Ball 1990a). As we noted earlier, this contrasts starkly with the virtual exclusion of union and local authority representatives from arenas of influence and the much diminished and discredited contribution from the educational establishment.

This context of influence has a symbiotic but none the less uneasy relation to the second context, the *context of policy text production*. Because while influence is often related to the articulation of narrow interests and dogmatic ideologies, policy texts are normally articulated in the language of general public good. Their appeal is based upon claims to popular (and populist) commonsense and political reason. Policy texts therefore *represent* policy. These representations can take various forms: most obviously 'official' legal texts and policy documents; also formally and informally produced commentaries which offer to 'make sense of' the 'official' texts, again the media is important here; also the speeches by and public performances of relevant politicians and officials; and 'official' videos are another recently popular medium of representation. Many of those towards whom policy is aimed rely on these secondhand accounts as their main source of information and understanding of policy as intended. But two key points have to be made about these ensembles of texts which represent policy. First, the ensembles and the individual texts are not necessarily internally coherent or clear. The expression of policy is fraught with the possibility of misunderstanding, texts are generalized, written in relation to idealizations of the 'real world', and can never be exhaustive, they cannot cover all eventualities. The texts can often be contradictory (compare National Curriculum statutory guidance with NCC produced Non-Statutory Guidance), they use key terms differently, and they are reactive as well as expository (that is to say, the representation of policy changes in the light of events and circumstances and feedback from arenas of practice). Policy is not done and finished at the legislative moment, it evolves in and through the texts that represent it, texts have to be read in relation to the time and the particular site of their production. They also have to be read with and against one another – intertextuality is important. Second, the texts themselves are the outcome of struggle and compromise. The control of the representation of policy is problematic. Control over the timing of the publication of texts is important. A potent and immediate example of struggle in arenas of text production is that which goes on (as noted already) in relation to National Curriculum working party reports (Ball 1990a). The interchange of documents between the NCC, SEAC and the DES is also a case in point. Groups of actors working within different sites of text production are in competition for control of the representation of policy. Most of these struggles go on behind closed doors but occasional glimpses of the dynamics of conflict are possible. What is at stake are attempts to control the meaning of policy through its representation.

Policies then are textual interventions but they also carry with them material constraints and possibilities. The responses to these texts have 'real' consequences. These consequences are experienced within the third main context, the *context of practice*, the arena of practice to which policy refers, to which it is addressed.

The key point is that policy is not simply received and implemented within this arena rather it is subject to interpretation and then 'recreated'. The exact same point is made by Rizvi and Kemmis (1987, p.21) in their analysis of the Victoria Participation and Equity Programme:

> Those who participate in a program at the school level will interpret it in their own terms, in relation to their own understanding, desires, values and purposes, and in relation to the means available to them and the ways of working they prefer. In short, all aspects of a program may be *contested* by those involved in a program, moreover, a program is formed and reformed throughout its life through a process of contestation.

Practitioners do not confront policy texts as naive readers, they come with histories, with experience, with values and purposes of their own, they have vested interests in the meaning of policy. Policies will be interpreted differently as the histories, experiences, values, purposes and interests which make up any arena differ. The simple point is that policy writers cannot control the meanings of their texts. Parts of texts will be rejected, selected out, ignored, deliberately misunderstood, responses may be frivolous, etc. Furthermore, yet again, interpretation is a matter of struggle. Different interpretations will be in contest, as they relate to different interests (Ball 1987), one or other interpretation will predominate, although deviant or minority readings may be important. Rizvi and Kemmis (1987, p.29) again underline this point:

> Because the participants in the contests which shape the evolution of a program start from different positions of relative power, the program, as it emerges, is disorted by the exercise of power, and freezes certain dominant ways of thinking into its structure.

But we must not see power in relation to policy as a fixed dimension. In patterns of contestation claims to power will always be tested in process, power is an outcome. Rizvi and Kemmis (1987, p.28) also make the important point that contestation is not a problem as such, it should not be seen as untoward or extraordinary:

Processes of contestation should not be thought to be unusual, and certainly not reprehensible. In fact contestation is a perfectly usual means through which ideas are developed and tested. In social life in general, different ideas, practices and forms of organization all have their advocates, and the evolution of social forms takes place through a struggle between supporters of different positions.

In all this authoritative interpretations may be at a premium. For many practitioners their response to texts will be constructed on the basis of 'interpretations of interpretations' (Rizvi and Kemmis 1987, p.14). In a similar way the evaluation of policy in practice or of practitioner responses will be the outcome of contested interpretations. Evaluation is a way of making sense of practice for particular purposes. The definition of those purposes and the control or the machinery of evaluation are what is important. Thus it seems far more appropriate to talk of policies as having 'effects' rather than 'outcomes'. The policy process is one of complexity, it is one of policy-making and remaking. It is often difficult, if not impossible to control or predict the effects of policy, or indeed to be clear about what those effects are, what they mean, when they happen. Clearly, however interpretations are not infinite, clearly also, as noted already, different material consequences derive from different interpretations in action. Practitioners will be influenced by the discursive context within which policies emerge. Some will have an eye to personal or localized advantage, material or otherwise, which may stem from particular readings of policy texts. But to reiterate, the meanings of texts are rarely unequivocal. Novel or creative readings can sometimes bring their own rewards. New possibilities can arise when 'national' policies intersect with local initiatives. Equally, as we shall see, different aspects of the same policy ensemble may contradict to the extent that certain well established readings of texts may have very different consequences and implications for practice.

Chapter 2

Education in the marketplace

As of 1 April 1990 many state-funded schools in England and Wales formally took control of their own budgets under the LMS (Local Management of Schools) provisions of the Education Reform Act 1988. At the same time Open Enrolment was introduced and the phasing in of per capita related funding of schools was begun. In effect a quasi-market in education was established.

The issue of the influence of markets on public sector welfare provision and in education in particular is one of the most important research topics of the 1990s. The Government's legislation programme has created a 'natural experiment' that presents researchers with an extraordinary opportunity to study the constitution and effect of market forces upon public service organizations. We suggest that the LMS/market package for schools rests upon two closely interrelated bases, (1) The neo-liberal economic theories of the market, particularly the work of Friedrich Hayek and his fellow Austrians; (2) recent developments in management theory and business methods which rest on a belief in achieving greater effectiveness through financial delegation; which, it is argued, provides for greater responsiveness to clients. The Peters and Waterman (1982) book *In Search of Excellence* is a key text here. The delegation argument contends that those actively engaged in delivering the service to the client are best placed to decide how to use resources most effectively and efficiently. It is important to underline the inter-relation between these two bases. Government strategies for changing schools clearly link the use of market forces with the reform of school management. The former changes the basis of the consumers' relation to the school. The latter changes the means and medium of the producers' response. In terms of political philosophy and economic theory freedom is thus linked to effectiveness and the result is system change.

The theory of markets in particular has been sponsored and advanced by a number of neo-liberal think tanks, research groups and advisers who have been influential in recent Conservative Party policy making. And a number of influential politicians, including Keith Joseph and Rhodes Boyson, both avowed followers of Hayekian economics have played a major part inside Government and inside the Conservative Party over the past 15 years in arguing the relevance of markets for the education system (see Ball 1990a). Market theory, Austrianism as it is sometimes known, rests upon a set of relatively straightforward premises which link market functions, and particularly competition, to individual choice. It is a form of reductive micro-economics. Reekie (1984, p.37) explains the dynamic of the theory as follows:

> The competitive process provides incentives and so evokes effort. It generates a continuous and universal search for substitutes, for ways of replacing the less desirable by the more desirable. This process of substitution begins with the consumer seeking to distribute his income to best advantage and passes on to the producer the striving to replace the less by the more sought after goods and substituting a better way of producing for a worse way. The essence of the whole process is choice by the consumer; emulation, rivalry and substitution by the producer.

The market is conceived of as 'no more than an exchange process' (Barry 1987, p.33). An exchange process in which all parties benefit. The market itself is taken to be neutral, simply a mechanism, an unplanned outcome of myriad choices. It is not necessarily fair or equal, indeed if it did generate equality it would remove incentive and competitive drive. For Hayek and his followers at the Institute of Economic Affairs, the market is always preferable to and superior to any form of partisan, value-driven state planning. The market empowers, 'frees', the consumer and provides incentive for the producer. It ensures progress and technological development as the entrepreneur searches for new products and cheaper production processes. Thus, the ethical value of free choice is combined with the effect of efficiency in the allocation of resources. The key question here is whether the processes of choice, exchange, emulation, rivalry and substitution do or might operate in these ways in the education market.

One basic assumption in this conception of market dynamics is that of purposive action. The idea that individuals consciously act in order to achieve chosen goals. Von Mises (1976, p.34) asserts that: 'action is purposive conduct. It is not simply behaviour, but behaviour begot by judgements of value, aiming at a definite end and guided by ideas concerning the suitability or unsuitability of definite means.' In other words a great deal here rests upon the assumption of active, informed and selective choice-making of, in this case, parents (as consumers) and entrepreneurial action on the part of school managers (as producers). The function of the entrepreneur being to seek out opportunities in the market before others perceive them. But Austrianism takes this one stage further. The result of the aggregate of individual consumer choices is order, equilibrium, a kind of social discipline. This is because, it is argued, under appropriate conditions the knowledge and intentions of different consumers move into agreement, their expectations of entrepreneurs, both subjective and objective, come together. Market equilibrium assumes that objective and subjective knowledge are reconciled. It could be argued that the system of national assessment and testing of students is an attempt to impose or facilitate this kind of equilibrium in education by providing authoritative data on producer effectiveness. *The National Curriculum 5–16 Consultation Document* asserts that national testing will:

Enable teachers to be more accountable for the education they offer to their pupils individually and collectively. The governing body, headteacher and the teachers of every school will be better able to undertake the essential process of regular evaluation because they will be better able to consider their school, taking account of its particular circumstances, against the local and national picture as a whole ... parents will be able to judge their children's progress against agreed national targets for attainment and also will be able to judge the effectiveness of their school.

(DES 1987, para 9 (ii))

However, in the creation of this kind of centrally determined accountability a key assumption of choice theory is short-circuited in so far as government imposition of testing both pre-empts the goals and beliefs of the individual consumer and may in fact constrain or construct for the consumer notions of what counts as 'good' or 'desirable' forms of education. Perversely, this smacks of the sort of paternalism that Austrianism seeks to root out. But this in turn points to one of the major weaknesses of Austrian praxedogy. The idea of free choice or goal-directed individual choice can only be preserved by ignoring those factors which influence or construct choices in the interests of the pro-ducers (like advertising) or the Government (like propaganda, control of the media etc.). There is no room here for ideas like ideology. Thus, Barry (1987, p.51) argues that 'although it is true that producers will try to influence individuals this effort will only be one of a whole congeries of factors which go to make up the act of consumption'. But even if we were to exempt national testing from criticisms of this sort it is still questionable whether this sort of information fulfils the requirement for full, perfect and instantaneous data that rational expectations theory requires if individuals are to adjust their expectations 'correctly'. In other words, it is reasonable to suggest that either there is an infor-mation shortfall in education; or we do not know enough about the reasons parents choose schools for their children; or Austrianism is wildy over-rational in its conception of the consumer when applied to this field. Meyer (1986, p.62) makes the point that: 'Modern economics models man as a choosing machine that is able to use available resources optimally in order to get the most utility.' In terms of education, Edwards and Whitty (1990) suggest that this means treating the ideal parent as the average parent. And this does not seem to align very closely with what little we do know about how parents actually choose their children's schooling (MacBeth et al. 1986; Stillman and Maychell 1986). However, not all economists subscribe to this view of choice as 'individualistic rational calculus' (IRC). Sen (1982) for example, is able to demonstrate that assumptions of IRC employed by micro-economic, public choice theorists rarely obtain in the real world in relation to imperfect markets. He also challenges the assumption of universal rationalism and refuses to accept a view of the world as populated by what he calls 'rational fools' and 'social morons'.

The theoretical market is thus constituted by three elements; the individual choices of consumers; the reactive and proactive strategies of producers and their constant adjustment of their 'commodity offering' and the order or equilibrium which is thus produced. Thus far research in education has made some inroads into the nature of parental choice, although the significance of the new political and financial context for schools means that the findings from previous research should not be simply carried over. But there is little or no work reported on the entrepreneurial behaviour of schools or on the effects or outcomes, the order, of the market.

This chapter is primarily concerned with these last two aspects of the education market and consists of some informed discussion, some questions for further research and the presentation of data from our case-study research. We look first at schools as entrepreneurs (see also Chapter 3).

SCHOOLS AS ENTREPRENEURS

As indicated earlier the key assumption made by the Conservative Government in its policies on school financing is that a combination of self-management and market forces will produce significant improvements in the quality of state education. That is, self-management will ensure that schools are able to match their services directly to student need and that market forces will ensure that 'standards' are raised as schools compete for students and seek to stabilize or maximize their income. 'Local management is about making schools more responsive to parents' needs as well as more effective in meeting them' (DES 1988b). As we shall see below in certain respects this set of linkages *does* occur in practice. But we will also indicate that the relationships between educational objectives and marketing can also be contradictory in practice. The ways in which schools conceptualize their markets and their market strategies do not always rest upon matching their services to student need. The priorities of the market and of educational planning are not automatically compatible. Neither, as most texts and official documents imply, is the marketing of education value-free, merely a technical matter.

Furthermore, the case for devolved budgets and decentralized decision-making – the self-managing school – often fails to connect the discussion of budgetary control to the realities of budgetary allocation and inter-school competition. There is also a degree of self-delusion involved in the notion that budgetary control is somehow liberating and inevitably more efficient without attention to the simple but crucial question of the size of the budget. LEA control of the size of the General Schools Budget and Government controls over LEA spending via the central spending estimates and poll-capping are major sources of constraint and of inequality. What is more, most writers seem to conveniently ignore the fact that student recruitment is inelastic, the student population is fixed. Increases in the roll of one school can only be achieved by decreases elsewhere. Greater budgetary flexibility in one school will mean additional constraints and a reduction in services in another. This is already happening as historic budgets are adjusted in relation to current levels of recruitment. Many schools are starting out by losing cash.

The DES seem to be assuming that movement between schools, as a result of Open Enrolment will be marginal, 5–10 per cent of parents. But equally they expect some schools to close (see Ball 1990a). Obviously the most dramatic possibilities for the effects of market forces and competition exist in those areas where there is a significant surplus of school places. (We return to the issues of movements of choice and school closures below.)

The texts on LMS/LFM (local financial management) typically treat the market issue with a mixture of apolitical naivety and wishful thinking. For example, Fidler (1989, p.18) notes that 'Market research, i.e. knowing what parents think about schools and what they want of schools, is likely to be an expanded activity. However, true marketing, that is adapting the way schools operate to fulfil the wishes of parents clearly would be much more problematic and would have to be balanced against the professional judgements of teachers about the needs of children.' Has this 'problematic' not been at the heart of what much of the politics of education of the last 20 years has been about? The Conservative/Black Paper distrust of teachers and the Hayekian attack upon the autonomy of state professionals provides one of the main ideological planks for current legislation. What is this 'balance' he refers to and how is the weight of 'professional judgement' to be determined? Also we might ask where schools, which are losing cash in the adjustment of budgets, are expected to find the money to fund their market research. Fidler then goes on to acknowledge that educational planning and the setting of organizational objectives in these 'new times', (what he calls formulating a strategy) is related not simply to educational priorities, 'Not surprisingly strategy in business thinking is very bound up with competition' (pp.23–4). He seems to want it both ways, 'professional judgement' provides 'balance' but competition is inescapable. We return to this tension below (see also chapter 6).

In the case of state schools, where at present the use of price as a basis for competition is unavailable, Fidler suggests that competition will be driven by 'differentiation'. If there are a number of attributes that are widely valued by consumers then means of differentiation 'may go beyond just carrying out the basic organisational task better. It may be achieved by the way that the organisation goes about the task, or by its marketing approach.' Thus, schools may seek to specialize, some kind of niche-marketing, (as Wandsworth LEA has tried to encourage its secondary schools to do, unsuccessfully), or employ particular marketing strategies. An interesting and novel example of this is provided by Ponteland County High School (see Fig. 2.1). Ponteland's market strategy is based on academic performance in public examinations but also employs a version of price as a factor in competition. But competition here is with the private sector. In seeking to maximize its intake Ponteland is attempting to attract parents away from private schools. (Again we return to the role of the private sector below.) But Fidler's passing and tentative references to marketing are in contrast to the discussion in another paper in the same collection by his co-editor Bowles. 'Marketing professionals', he argues:

> Would insist that marketing should be seen as integral to the management role of any enterprise operating in a competitive environment and be a total strategy starting from the aims and objectives of the organisation, feeding into its information and decision-making systems and being closely connected to monitoring, evaluation and staff development activities.
>
> (Bowles 1989, p.38)

Here there seems to be no prevarication, it must be the market which determines the setting of aims and objectives and the processes of decision-making. Professional judgement here is reserved for the marketer and entrepreneur rather than any educationalist concern with matching services to needs. As Dale (1989) points out 'needs' do not sit easily in a planning system driven by demands of efficiency. And the easy and common

```
┌─────────────────────────────────────────┐
│              Private                     │
│             Education                    │
└─────────────────────────────────────────┘
```

```
╔═══════════════════════════════════════════╗
║                                           ║
║   Worried about the Education             ║
║      of your children?                    ║
║                                           ║
║   Summer 1989 statistics:                 ║
║   91% pass rate at A-level                ║
║   68.7% pass rate at grades A, B or C at A-level  ║
║   65% pass rate at A-level General Studies (compulsory for all students)  ║
║                                           ║
║   66 University places and 20 Polytechnic places from an  ║
║              upper sixth of 110           ║
║   A leading independent school – fees £2,800 p.a.?  ║
║                                           ║
║              No!                          ║
║   PONTELAND COUNTY HIGH SCHOOL            ║
║         fees £0.00 p.a.                   ║
║                                           ║
║   A number of places are available in September 1990 to students  ║
║   from outside our catchment area: a preliminary meeting for  ║
║   interested parents will be held in the school at 7.30 on  ║
║   February 8th 1990.                      ║
║   Please ring Mrs Bell on 0681 24711 Ext. 201 if you are  ║
║   interested in attending.                ║
║                                           ║
╚═══════════════════════════════════════════╝
```

Figure 2.1 Newspaper advertisement for Ponteland School

conflation of efficiency with effectiveness only serves to obscure basic differences in organizational conduct and intent. Politicians and advocates of self-management regularly deploy this conflation for rhetorical purposes.

Bowles goes on to argue that marketing begins with a policy, a statement of intent, or a 'mission statement'. And adds that:

> This will in itself be a developmental process and is a necessary part of both the budgetary and the marketing processes which are interlinked . . . If the activity of marketing is seen as the

continuing search for sustainable competitive advantage then the process becomes one of reconciling goals with resources, an interactive exercise in matching the ideal against the possible.

(p.40)

The problem here for us is that again the weight or significance of the elements, the statement of educational objectives, budgetary considerations, and marketing considerations remains unclear. What seems to be suggested is that 'sustainable competitive advantage' can be reconciled fairly unproblematically with some kind of professionally determined agenda of priorities. But this is not necessarily the case. Fidler's initial coyness is replaced by Bowles clear restatement of Conservative policy and Hayekian theory. Establishing a mission:

Begins by establishing clearly whose needs the school is there to serve. It has been too producer-dominated, too concerned with serving its own ends and imposing its own views on its clients. The present changes are designed to make the system more responsive, more answerable to the customer.

(p.40)

So much for professional judgement! This kind of 'nonconsequentialist moral reasoning' is basic to much advocacy of the market (IPPR 1991). But Bowles goes on to another key question. Who is the client or customer? The parent? The student? It is not as simple as that.

A more sophisticated and more honest answer recognizes the range of clients and objectives a school has and acknowledges the relative power they each have to influence the school's activities and tries to accommodate this in a plan of priorities for action.

(p.4)

Here again the fiction of market freedom and mutual benefit seems to come unstuck. The maximizing of their wellbeing by some here would seem to involve the potential reduction in wellbeing of others; 'decisions by one family "spill over" and both affect and constrain the choices of other families' (IPPR 1991, p.3). The assumption of 'man as assiduous calculator' (Barry 1987, p.52) would seem to ignore the uneven distribution of skills involved in making choices, and differences in power or ability in making those choices 'felt' (see Ball 1990b). The idea of schools responding to their clients has to be related to Knight's (1976, p.2) point in relation to the ethics of competition that: 'The inheritance of wealth, culture, educational advantage and economic opportunity tend toward the progressive increase of opportunity' and Mackenzie's (1987, p.16) assertion that 'the market system is a means of distributing power among people and for getting things done'. This relates to what Brown (1990, p.66) calls the 'ideology of parentocracy', 'where a child's education is increasingly dependent upon the wealth and wishes of parents, rather than the ability and efforts of pupils'. Thus, again there is a basic tension between a needs-led analysis and market-driven responsiveness. Is it enough to satisfy the needs of those who drive the market, the DES's estimated 5–10 per cent? Or should schools have a wider public welfare, public service, brief?

According to Bowles' scenario the way forward for schools is via external and internal audits. The former is an assessment of trends, constraints, possibilities and demands. The latter is a review of institutional strengths and weaknesses. This should then lead 'to the identification of the USP (the Unique Selling Proposition) – that particular thing or blend of things that your school can offer in a way that gives it a differential advantage over its competitors' (1989, p.41). Here again we seem to have come along way from the idea of 'matching services to student need' (Caldwell and Spinks 1988, p.6). And thus some important slippages are achieved within the discourse of marketing and management. The notions of educational judgement based on professional or research criteria and of value judgement or value dispute are almost totally displaced. They have no standing. They are indicted as part of the 'producer interest' and a barrier to choice. The customer/parent always knows best, a further aspect of Brown's 'ideology of parentocracy'. Thus, Bowles suggests that 'In deciding what to do it will be important to consider the marketing value of the offerings as well as their educational merits' (1989, p.42). And

> In marketing terms any activity can be seen as potentially either an earner of cash or credit or a loser of either or both. Painful decisions will have to be faced as to whether the return on a given activity justifies the expenditure it incurs in terms of time, effort or money. Schools will have to become more

skilled in making assessments of the benefits of their activities
in term of return in relation to cost and/or in terms of gain in
client estimation.

(pp. 42–3)

Where are the educational merits here?

Throughout the body of literature and rhetoric related to LMS
in schools there is a division and a tension between those arguments which privilege the market and see the ERA as empowering consumers and others which privilege organizational
autonomy and see the ERA as empowering school managers. The
question now is which arguments and what imperatives are
being taken most seriously by schools? Are schools becoming
market-oriented in their planning and decision-making? Are
there real changes taking place in the nature of organizational
control and dominant values in schools – 'the new culture and
ethos of organisation' as the Coopers and Lybrand (1988) Report
on LMS puts it. Basically, we know little as yet about how
education markets work or what sort of 'new order' they will
produce. It is certainly dangerous to read off the workings and
effects of social markets from those of commercial markets. Le
Grand (1990) calls these developments quasi-markets:

> They are 'markets' because they replace monolithic state pro-
> viders with competitive independent ones. They are 'quasi'
> because they differ from conventional markets in a number of
> key ways. The differences are on both the supply and the
> demand sides. On the supply side, as with conventional
> markets, there is competition between productive enterprises
> or service suppliers. Thus, in all the schemes described there
> are independent institutions (schools, universities, hospitals,
> residential homes, housing associations, private landlords)
> competing for customers. However, in contrast to conven-
> tional markets, these organisations are not necessarily out to
> maximise their profits; nor are they necessarily privately
> owned. Precisely what such enterprises maximise, or could be
> expected to maximise, is unclear, as is their ownership
> structure.
>
> (p.5)

Le Grand's definition of quasi-markets serves to underline one of
the key themes of our analysis of education policy in this volume.

That is the presence of ambiguity, contradictions and general incoherence that become evident when schools attempt to translate national policies into practice. In the case of markets that incoherence arises in relation to the status and purposes of the independent institutions (schools) which constitute the supply side of the market. As we shall see, our case study schools work with many doubts, concerns and uncertainties with regard to competition and the market. Furthermore, the analysis of the engagement of these schools in 'the market' makes it very clear that there is no one 'market in education' and no one set of market conditions. Schools operate in relation to multiple markets, usually local, which have very specific conditions, constraints and histories. Importantly too schools are increasingly finding themselves implicated in other markets and their attendant regulatory legislation, e.g. the leisure, financial and labour markets, each of which impinges upon the other and upon the 'educational markets' that emerge out of local responses to the ERA.

MARKET DYNAMICS AND THE POLITICS OF SPACE

Education markets and other quasi-markets in the social welfare sector have some characteristics that are closer to the service sector of the private economy than to the manufacturing or financial sectors. One such characteristic is the importance of space or geography, and, in relation to this, 'locality'. Massey (1984) makes our point here very succinctly:

> Geography matters. The fact that processes take place over space, the facts of distance or closeness, of geographical variation between areas, of the individual character and meaning of specific places and regions – all these are essential to the operation of social processes themselves. Just as there are no purely spatial processes, neither are there any non-spatial social processes . . . Geography . . . is not a constraint on a pre-existing non-geographical social and economic world. It is constitutive of that world.
>
> (pp. 52–3)

Consequently we have to come to grips with at least three conceptual aspects of space in relation to the market. The first is the historical construction of locality and community which situates schools physically and cognitively in relation to certain groups of potential consumers. How do parents and students view their local area in terms of the available schools? Are schools 'identified' with their locality? How and to what extent does this change over time? The second, is the socially constructed limits and possibilities of the market conceived of by the producers, the manipulation of demand. How do schools view their potential consumers and what activities do they undertake to attract them? What impact do LEA policies have upon demand, for example the number of school places in relation to the number of students? The third, are the practical and physical constraints imposed by transport facilities, road networks and traffic flows and the various barriers to movement. These three are, in practice, powerfully interrelated.

To a great extent the rhetoric of quasi-markets ignores these 'realities' of competition and choice. And certainly, as regards the first, the theory of the market actually sets itself *against* school–community relations by privileging the relations between schools and individual consumers. Paradoxically this attempt to break the link between locality and school via the market may actually fly in the face of parental choice. After all a crucial factor that is reiterated in all the major British studies of choice of school is proximity. For large numbers of parents a very high priority is placed upon the nearness of a school (Alder *et al.* 1989, MacBeth, *et al.* 1986, Stillman and Maychell 1986). Clearly for some parents the crude indicators of standards noted above, or concerns over reputations or status *are* important when choosing schools, *but not for all*. Stillman and Maychell make the simple but important point that most parents give a combination of reasons for choice of school, but only 54 per cent in their sample gave any 'product' reasons (like examination results) when explaining their choice of school. Thus we need to recognize that space is important in relation to choice and that choice is both diverse and complex.

In considering Massey's second area of interest we would point to the LEA as one of the producers of socially constructed limits and possibilities within the educational market. Here we have in mind the LEA's capacity, now significantly diminished, to manipulate school admission numbers and to supervise the parental appeals procedure for choices of secondary school. (We go on to look at the former in more detail in the next section.)

In every respect the third conceptual area in Massey's work, the practical and physical as constraints on freedoms for the operation of markets, is the most neglected. Here again matters of choice are informed by matters of possibility or constraint. The lived environment is not equally available to all, it is classed, it is gendered and it is racially grounded (Ball 1990b, Jonathan 1990).

THE LOCAL HISTORY OF EDUCATION MARKETS

In the two local authorities with which we are concerned recent local history has helped to produce particular market orientations among the secondary schools. In Westway it is generally acknowledged that there is 'one secondary school too many'.

> The council elected not to close or amalgamate two schools, therefore they're going to be operating with 14 secondary schools and a considerable surplus of secondary places in the authority. That surplus of places will look bad as far as the DES is concerned. Therefore the next move by the authority now is to reduce the number of places in secondary schools in the LEA. Now they can do this by closing down wings of schools, which is quite difficult, because within a wing you may have different classrooms and laboratories and whatever, and therefore relocate some of them.
>
> (Senior Deputy, Parkside school, 5 July 1989)

The LEA has never quite been able to bring itself to select one school for closure. Ironically it may well be the fear among local politicians of parental reaction to the closure of their 'local' school, reflected at the ballot box, that produces this unwillingness. Whether this fear is parental choice in heavy disguise is something of a moot point. However, the outcome is a climate for schools to enter into competition for that relatively scarce commodity, the student. While it may well be that market forces result in the closure of one of the schools in Westway, that is by no means certain.

Riverway is also interesting in this respect. In Riverway two factors seem to have been, and look set to remain, important. First, over the last ten years 20–26 per cent of secondary age children living in the authority have been educated in the independent sector. (The figure has been more favourable to the state sector since Riverway went comprehensive!) Second, 30 per cent of the secondary age children in the LEA schools come from outside the LEA boundary. This means that school enrolments while buoyant also have a certain fragility. The competitive relations between the LEA schools, with the independent sector and with schools in other LEAs are heightened as a result. The Riverway Director of Education makes this clear:

> To some extent Riverway schools have always had to be fairly competitive, because when you started, well in secondary schools, when you had falling rolls about ten years ago there wasn't a decision to rationalise, and we've maintained our number of schools by importing from neighbouring Boroughs, to a large extent because of the position of the schools in the Borough because they tend to be on the periphery of the Borough. The schools are not competing with each other for the Borough pupils, they've got their own kind of territories in that sense and they've all had to be kind of quite strongly into marketing to survive anyway, if you think about it. So all the schools in the past have been quite attuned to marketing, they tend to market for other Borough pupils in different areas, personally I don't think there's been a lot of change because of the nature of this LEA.
>
> (4 September 1990)

In the recent past then, it has been the LEAs, unprepared to close down schools, that have created the opportunity for market conditions to flourish. Consequently, while the ERA has created a new financial context for competition between schools by linking market performance directly to institutional survival, and attempting to give a new legitimacy to competitive activities, competition between schools is not new. Falling rolls over the past 15 years have resulted in thousands of schools being closed and hundreds amalgamated, yet in many parts of the country a surplus of places still exists (Bondi 1989). Such surpluses are likely to be a central factor in the dynamics of education markets. Thus, some of the data on competition and marketing reported below have a history that goes back well beyond the ERA of 1988. Although the discourse of markets provides one way of conceptualizing this history, it has to be recognized that within the provisions of the 1988 Act such a discourse is employed as one means of giving that history new teeth. Consequently, while we do not intend to understate the impact of per capita funding and the removal of LEA controls over enrolments on schools and on the orientations of headteachers, neither do we want to suggest an absolute break with the past.

There is little doubt that prior to the 1988 Act the LEAs took political decisions about the numbers of students each school would accommodate. Whatever the grounds of such decisions this option is no longer the province of the LEAs, numbers are fixed by the 1979 standard intake for each school. This removal of local autonomy is carefully calculated to privilege the market by setting individual school numbers at a particularly high level. The intention is to promote a situation, evident in the authorities above, in which the number of places is greater than the number of students. Thus the deliberate manipulation of place numbers versus student population is clearly political, for both the LEA and the Government. It is but one aspect of market dynamics which tends to focus attention upon the nature of competition. (At the same time the Audit Commission continues to press for LEA policies to reduce spare capacity.) However, it is important to recognize that market dynamics are a good deal more complex than this.

'READING' THE LOCAL MARKET(S)

While the ERA sets out to increase 'consumer power' it remains incumbent upon the supply side (schools) to reflect this demand in their planning. We want to give some indication of the ways in which producers conceive of their market position and their 'reading' of consumer preferences and requirements. In part this is a matter of the social make-up of client groups, in part the possibilities and limitations of catchment areas, and in part who your competitors are. Pankhurst, the girls' school, clearly sees the independent sector as providing the major competition.

> Yes, yes I can do, but the numbers are very satisfactory at the moment, we've got our numbers for next year, so we're very happy about that. We're over-subscribed. What happens here, I don't know if I told you, is families double book with us and with independent schools and then when they get into an independent school they withdraw, so I always have to have 50 or 60 extra pupils, to guarantee an entry of 180.
>
> (Head of Pankhurst, 28 November 1989)

The Riverway area and the area around Pankhurst has a particularly high density of independent schools, which reflects, across the LEA and in the surrounding districts, a high level of parental wealth.

> Oh yes, there's Lady of the Lake, there's Muffets, there's Goldseal, and there's St Simon's. All those you see are within travelling distance and, that's four, and there's Puckeridge High, there's Winston High all possible. Puckeridge High hasn't quite such a good reputation but people think it's good. Well that's quite a lot of schools as well of course as the people who actually want boarding.
>
> (Head of Pankhurst, 28 November 1989)

But in the past this has not been a matter of Pankhurst alone competing with the independent schools.

> With the independent schools it's difficult, isn't it. The LEA as a whole is trying to promote the Riverway experience, you know, primary through to tertiary, very stable schools. We haven't had big alterations, and I mean Riverway is, the schools are, very pleasant places to come into. We advertise as an LEA and we do a little bit of private advertising as well. I don't quite know, a lot will depend on the primary Heads and some take that more seriously than others. Some families of course are just determined to have independent education.
>
> (Head of Pankhurst, 28 November 1989)

In order to ensure that the local schools were kept open (see earlier) the LEA has had to actively promote the state schools and is unusual (though not unique) in deliberately seeking to attract so many students from other LEAs. Under the terms of the ERA the responsibility for marketing lies far more with the individual schools than the LEA and it remains to be seen whether Pankhurst will be increasingly left on its own to compete with other girls' schools in other LEAs and the independent schools. Our data suggest that the independents seem to have a wide catchment area that extends across several LEA boundaries and strongly reflects parental ability to provide transport for their children; not to mention pay the school fees. For a large 'core' of the Pankhurst parents this option is not available and a local school must suffice. The Head was asked about attracting girls in from a distance.

Not really. We're growing, we get girls from Westway now and we are getting some from the Chiselworth area, 'cos there's one bus comes directly. But it's a long way, Chiselworth to Pankhurst. We get two or three every year from the Chiselworth area, and we're now up to roughly 30 a year from Westway and about once a year we get somebody from Queensway. But I think people in Queensway think Riverway is a long way away, again you can sit on one bus.

(28 November 1989)

Which 'bits' of the market will Pankhurst need to appeal to in order to keep up its overall numbers? What is evident here is two distinct markets and sets of market relationships both based upon the attractiveness of single sex schooling for girls, or at least the connotations of single sex. Here single sex also stands for and partly signifies tradition and standards. Competition with the local independent girls' schools is one thing, and travel restrictions and distance seem of minor importance, the cross-LEA competition between state girls' schools is another, and here travel plays some part at least. But in this already fairly complex relationship of status, type, reputation and accessibility other factors, like ethnicity and class, interact with gender in differentiating between schools. The Head of English at Pankhurst had previously taught at a rival girls' school which loses 20–30 of its local girls to Pankhurst every year, so she was able to draw some comparisons in terms of catchment and parental perceptions.

Who can say. I mean, so obviously they feel they will get a better education here, but I mean who can say why that is. Reputations of schools are built on very different things, aren't they? . . . I think the Penworth group of girls are coming here, because it's quite easy to get here from Penworth, as easy as it is to get to Tomsford, and I think, I wouldn't like to say really, because I think there are so many factors that influence parents to change their daughters' school. Well there are better results here, and there's no question about that. There is a more middle class intake here, so there's a better balance in a way of social groups . . . Tomsford draws from the local area, which is mainly white working class and also Asian girls from Westway, who of course also can get here as easily as they can to Tomsford and I think, although there were very many positive things going on there I think really it is, I should imagine the results are a major factor.

(28 November 1989)

Pankhurst is a *cosmopolitan* school if we may use that term to refer to a geographically diverse catchment. In contrast Flightpath is very much a *local* school, as one of the senior teachers observed:

> Yes, there's an assumption though that children will travel, that students will travel, and there's an in-built resistance in this school, or in this community to travelling beyond a school, and the uptake is so small that I can't see that it would make a difference.
>
> (Senior teacher, Head of Sixth Form, Flightpath, 3 November 1989)

Thus choice-making around Flightpath is seen by the staff to be tied in part to the question of distance and even where Westway does lose students to Riverway this is viewed as a rational matter of selecting the closest school.

> Mmm, very few people in this area will go out, all right people do go to Riverside that are up towards the Chertwell Road, because over the road and you're in Riverside. But I mean, I don't think in a sense it's because they're rejecting us. I think that's part again of the attitude, well Chancel's nearer, it's a nearer school
>
> (Senior teacher, curriculum, Flightpath, 2 November 1989)

Flightpath thus appears to be locked into a local market which involves competing primarily with two other mixed comprehensive schools. In this competitive relationship Flightpath has both advantages and disadvantages. Its long-term reputation is a disadvantage. Size has also been a difficulty in its own right.

> We have a couple of other schools, (Chancel, which is outside the Borough) and they are smaller schools. One of the most offputting things that we've had to overcome in this school, is the size of the school, because when I came here, we were a 12-form entry, over 2,000 children, over 120-odd teaching staff, and parents coming from small primary schools . . . and if they were the quieter, meeker children, were very intimated . . . So we've had to work very hard at proving to them that big did not necessarily mean ugly and uncontrollable. Shortcross has

always been that little bit smaller than us, so again that worked
to their advantage at times although things have gone in
cycles. Crouchlands had the really good academic image and
to some extent still retains that, Shortcross and Flightpath had
the reputation of being very poor relations of the Borough,
both academically and behaviourwise. We came up the ladder,
partly because of the building project and the hard work that
went in, then Shortcross came up, now there's that sort of
balancing act going on the whole time.

(Senior teacher, Flightpath, 23 March 1990)

There is again an ethnic dimension to reputation and recruitment,
as well as a demographic shift. In Westway the early settlement
of Asian families was close to Crouchland, as this has dispersed
across the Borough so the Asian families have become part of the
potential catchment area of other schools. However, Flightpath
has been the subject of some activity from a locally based extreme
right wing organization and when set alongside the academic
and traditional reputation of a rival school this has led the
majority of local Asian parents to choose the latter.

No, there's certainly that, and there's something about, well
Flightpath itself has a history of being a very racist area, and
the Asian community hasn't actually impinged to any extent in
the immediate catchment of our school, the boundaries are,
but they go to Crouchland rather than come here, for the
obvious reasons. Crouchlands is slightly different from Flightpath and Shortcross, inasmuch as its intake is high ethnic
population and therefore they have this high profile of
academic achievement. And obviously the Asian parents tend
to give a far greater emphasis of support towards their
children at academic levels than say our intake or Shortcross's
intake.

(Head of Sixth Form, Flightpath, 23 March 1990)

On the plus side Flightpath has excellent facilities including
floodlit games pitches, a new sports hall and three computer
network suites. At this level it is not difficult to impress parents.
But the school certainly still feels the need to repackage and
present to potential parents its educational offerings. As we
discuss in Chapter 3, the school has taken the idea of marketing
very seriously:

That's why we've set up a marketing group, we've appointed someone, a teacher, on scale D, as school promotion manager, and I went along to a primary school to talk to third-year juniors last week, took a video, made a video of the school, and we're talking, sure as people talk in business, about what is the best way. I mean, we've been thinking that we ought to get closer to the pupils than to the parents actually in this respect, because we're told by headteachers in our partner schools that they often are the people that make the decisions, that put pressure on their parents. So we are thinking about that, very very seriously. But I mean at the end of the day, I'm much more anxious about whether we've got the product right, that we're promoting, that's what my real concern is. Because I get the feeling that if we get the product right it'll be relatively easy to promote the school.

(Senior Deputy, 17 July 1989)

The point here is that reputations can be made and lost, at least schools see that possibility.

There are reasons why our present fifth year is so small. There were rather unfortunate reasons. About six or seven years ago, we had very bad publicity about a fight which was a mile and a half from the school, but it was our girls in it – front page. And also this came at a time when the merger had finished and we had been fully subscribed, and we'd slipped a little bit. But we did no publicity, we sat on our laurels and thought people were going to came to Pankhurst and suddenly from 180 we got only 99 girls. Oh boy did we get the shock of our lives and we did take publicity very seriously, to get the name of the school really known. So it has taken about three years to overcome that.

(Head of Pankhurst, 28 November 1989)

Even the best recruiting schools seem to see dangers in complacency in the marketplace. And part of a marketing strategy involves 'targeting' potential clients. In some cases a particular primary school can become the focus of the attentions of competing secondaries. The Senior Deputy at Flightpath gave an example of this and the range of things that could be done as 'marketing'.

the primary Head might say, or the contact person might say 'we're very worried about a particular kid, where they're going, and we would like to direct them a little bit your way, because you've got a special needs department'. That sort of conversation. And sometimes we do a little more of a marketing exercise. Some years we've done more so than others. This basically consists of senior members of the school going round, they pick up a school each, and we go with a small video. A couple of days just going round the school, seeing the kids in different places. We would talk to their third year. And sometimes, to be honest, we have slightly heavier marketing, for example in the Smiths' Lane area, where we are competing with Chancel [a comprehensive in the adjacent LEA]. We don't really go for Shortcross [nearest comprehensive in the Westway LEA]. I mean Shortcross and us are competing for both markets, but I've never known it to be a particular issue about competing. But the Smiths' Lane area is very close to us, and it's pretty convenient for those kids. So if they're skipping over the boundary to Chancel, we have to ask questions about ourselves. So we have things like, a day for their third year in this school, and we give them a day's timetable in the school. So they get a taste of the school. We're doing it with another school this year. I wouldn't say it was a heavy marketing ploy.

(Senior Deputy, Flightpath, 2 May 1991)

All of this indicates the attention that schools do and have given to their market position. Brochures and videos are now the norm, the local press is used and cultivated to promote the image of schools where possible and bad press is avoided. Heads in particular spend a considerable amount of their time on activities related to public relations. But what we also see here is the complexity of the market and the different ways in which schools envisage their potential clients. There is certainly no one general education market that exists across LEAs or between communities in a particular locality. Rather there are a multitude of localized *and* specific market relations between groups or types of schools – micro-markets.

PROFIT MAXIMIZATION OR MARKET SHARE?

Clearly, attempts to find analogous forms in commerical markets and other pseudo-markets can be dangerous, but if we are to understand how pseudo-markets work then we need to identify the basis of competitive relations. Both advocates and critics of social markets have probably overestimated the extent to which individual schools will want to 'go for growth' as a strategy for maximizing income. In fact all of our case study schools actually developed and operated with a fairly well worked out sense of their 'optimum' or 'preferred' size. At Pankhurst this did involve some projected growth. One of the governors explained.

> What we want to try to do is to ensure that we get a larger number of children starting each year, than we have had over the last three or four years. At the moment the school numbers are, I think, somewhere in the region of 750 odd, and what we're looking for is 900. So we've got to go out 'marketing' to improve the number of inquiries, and then convert the inquiries as we would say, into actual applications and so forth. Actually then there's a subsidiary problem that we've got, a challenge that we face, and that is keeping them once they're accepted. 'Cos we get, at our particular school, a tremendous fall off from applications to children actually turning up on the first day and the numbers are such, as for example, I think last year, (I think this past year), September '89, no a bit earlier than that, maybe even in the June, we had something of the order of maybe 215 acceptances and we actually only had about 180 turn up. In fact we were full, it was very good, but there's a tremendous fall away, and that, in our particular case is of, we believe, children going into private education.
>
> (8 February 1990)

But the Senior Deputy at Parkside sees a tension between quality and size, between efficiency based upon numbers and effectiveness based on what is achieved, or the 'value-added'.

> It's all very well schools trying to get a large share of the market, but as they get a large share of the market and then can't deliver the goods, then they're going to find themselves in a very difficult and embarrassing position, and I think LMS originally was perhaps seen as a temptation for schools to become as large as they possibly could. But I think, yes, being large does provide a certain economy but it becomes more difficult to operate because your management costs might well escalate and you have to see what is the most effective level for

you. I've always maintained that we've been the wrong school, five-form entry school, 150, 155, standard number 155, then depressed artificially to 135 by the local authority, which is an awful number to try to manage really.

(5 July 1989)

A similar point is made by Adler *et al.* (1989). But, further, the calculation of optimum size, the possibilities of different target numbers, and the skills and difficulties involved in achieving these targets (not more nor less), once agreed, involve a complex institutional calculus, to say the least. The Senior Deputy at Parkside again:

Yes. Now under Open Enrolment we're allowed to go to our standard number, 155, and by the indicated number, 174 I think, and this poses some problems for us, if we've got 155 and keep it at five classes, five basic classes, say in first year, it means we have classes of over 30, which runs into union problems, as well as into problems, that is just as reasonable, in the classroom. If we try to break them down into six classes then we could find ourselves with some difficulty there of not quite having enough pupils to get the money to pay for the six teachers. If we were to go to the 174 I can see problems coming from overcrowding, because there are so many figures which become, loom very important in breaking down the school into manageable units. There's 30, the maximum class size which people will tolerate for long periods of time, there's this more hypothetical figure of 20 or so . . .

(27 November 1989)

So the optimum size, I reckon, is in the mid-160s to a year and if we work that through, I reckon if that's run for five years, we'd need something in the region of 38 teaching spaces at any one time. And we have got the facilities for that, and we've also got, just about got the right proportion of workshops, and so on, but it will need some redevelopment after about five years, to make sure, as these numbers progress in the sixth form, we can offer the full range of activities we should offer. So therefore we've got to get our building proposals in now for about four or five years' time.

(27 November 1989)

Here then the achievement of optimum size again requires some growth and investment in plant and facilities. However, as finance manager for his institution this deputy is also aware that any marketing difficulties and recruitment fluctuations will have a dramatic and immediate impact on the budget and thus on long-term planning. The budget will be determined year by year on the school roll. There is no hiding place, no fallback in this market. Schools are fully exposed to the vicissitudes of parental choice.

We're into a totally different game now, with Open Enrolment and the need to have a steady flow of pupils through the school. If we have hiccups one year and go down, that has immediate financial implications for the school. So we cannot afford (a) to get it wrong in the first place and (b) to have any hiccups or disasters along the way. In the past, with local government if there's a hiccup or something, then the impact has not been immediate on people. A hard luck story or something has been done to smooth it over. And I think the other thing which is crucial to us is our resources will be finite. In the past they haven't been infinite, but there has been a factor which enabled errors to creep in and be smoothed over, without any loss of face or loss of revenue and that is obviously going to disappear.

(27 November 1989)

The curriculum deputy at Flightpath gave a concrete example of such a 'hiccup' and the school's response.

It's a response to ethos, falling rolls and the market. We got a shock when we only had 195 applicants for our first year in September '89. We found out back in October, our response to that, with LMS and parental choice, now leads us to a position where we have to go out and advertise, we have to get the third year (primary students), the fourth years have already made their decision. The marketing side of that has gone along and we are advertising for an internal promotions manager.

(12 June 1989)

Another aspect of Flightpath's response to their 'shock' came in the form of a new approach to student groups and the monitoring of student performance. On the other hand there are problems involved in being full. In particular, there are problems about flexibility in timetabling and curriculum planning in relation to available accommodation. The Senior Deputy at Flightpath:

And this school on the whole has always been rather, well, in my experience, has always been rather tight on general classroom space. So the thought actually of going up to 270 is a bit worrying, I mean 270 through all five years we'd start having real problems because of the ratio of general classrooms to specialist. We'd be all right on specialist classrooms because the school took the opportunity, when it had the money to put into building, to build lots of specialist classrooms, so there's ten science labs for example, whereas there's only about an 8.3 usage of them. There were 10 CDT rooms with less than that, I mean, radically less, less than 50 per cent usage. I mean we closed, took out, two of the CDT rooms and converted them into general classrooms and in fact the general classrooms last year were operating at something like 95 per cent usage, which is really very difficult to timetable, and it meant that you couldn't give everybody their own room, there's a lot of people having to move about in different rooms. That's been eased a bit by the numbers falling and by the taking out of the CDT rooms, but obviously there is a space issue, that you kind of discuss. But there's no doubt about it that if you have some extra space to play with in a school, that's an advantage, there's lots of things you can do with extra space.

(1 December 1989)

And again the tension between size and effectiveness is raised. Again the rhetoric of the market has failed to address the issues involved in the impact of growth on quality in complex 'people-processing' institutions like schools. Popularity can have its drawbacks.

But if the quality of your education can be improved, that is going to affect your view of an optimum number, and your ability to recruit that optimum number, if you know what I mean, because if people then get to know that at that level school becomes less hectic, better organized, and so on, then it becomes popular, if you like, and I can see an ebb and flow situation could develop. You could become popular, but then become so crowded and hectic that you become unpopular, do you know what I mean, that sort of thing happens.

(1 December 1989)

The Head of Overbury talked about the considerable stresses involved, for her, in admissions issues, and the problem of never being able to 'get it right', having either too few students or too many. The year by year funding means that every admissions process becomes a cliff-hanger. If the school is over-subscribed one year then that message may discourage applications the next, if the school roll goes down then cuts may mean that it is impossible to stop the downward spiral. If the numbers grow too much, with appeals pushing numbers above a comfortable figure then standards and quality and image may suffer. Relationships with feeder primaries also become difficult; how much is good liaison? how much is manipulation? How long and how far can you hold to your principles? Values and ethics are under pressure, the centre is difficult to hold. The market allows for little in the way of principles. All of this then raises the question of how much time and energy and money to spend on the market? How much is enough? How much should you look over your shoulder at other schools? Will codes of practice hold. Will the collaboration with other schools hold or will someone 'opt out' or go all out for aggressive marketing?

TEACHERS IN THE MARKETPLACE

Within the Act teachers and LEAs are characterized as *producers* and the local community, industry and the parents/students, variously, as the *consumers*. Here we want to concentrate on the privileging of the consumer in the marketplace and we begin with parents as consumers.

> For example, we had an interesting meeting recently in which I was at the Parent Teachers Association, which generally is a fairly tame sort of thing, and then out of the blue somebody asked me a question unrelated to anything that I was prepared to talk about that evening, about whether anybody was doing mixed ability teaching under these new arrangements. And I happen to know that the English department decided to do mixed ability teaching in the lower school, and so I said yes, the English department, and if I'd have said they were considering child abuse, I probably wouldn't have had such a violent reaction as I got from that group of about 30 or 40 parents who attended that meeting. Unprepared for all this I

said, 'Look folks, I didn't actually make this particular decision. I do back it, support it, but if you really want to know more, you ought to meet the English department to talk about it'. So we've set up a meeting on Monday, which has all the makings of a first-rate row, because parents have marshalled themselves for the first time on any issue, apart from the building development which they've been very stroppy about one way or another, on this whole question of mixed ability in English. They've written to every parent and they've said, do you really want mixed ability in English and the English department feel as though there is some massive plot against them.

(Senior Deputy, Flightpath, 6 July 1989)

Parental questioning of teaching approaches has a long history that certainly predates the 1988 Act and although it appears to be a new phenomenon at Flightpath it would be quite wrong to infer the Act is giving rise to a wave of 'parent power'. Nonetheless, the beginnings of a change in institutional culture and in school/parent relations and the new operating context of the market do conspire to frame and inflect parental 'involvement' in new ways. In this case a public meeting was arranged where the English teachers and the LEA English adviser were required to put their case for mixed ability and attempt to convince the parents. One of the other deputies made it clear that his criterion for deciding on such matters was the presentation of a 'convincing argument' to the parents:

there are two things that can happen from that meeting, either English will convince the parents that . . . within mixed ability they can push every individual, which would be great, my personal convictions are not for mixed ability. I've seen some very good teachers teach it very well, but the average teacher struggles to cater for it. But I come from a maths/science background, so I would say that anyway. So excepting my personal bias, I am quite prepared, if they put a convincing argument for it, then fair enough, and convince the parents, then that's my criteria.

(Deputy Head, Flightpath, 12 June 1989)

There is a tension here between the traditional teacher profession-alism and the forces of the market as criteria for educational decision-making. A tension that senior staff were only too aware of.

> And I must admit, I'm in a divided situation here, because I do believe very fundamentally that teachers should have the right to decide the best way of organizing something to achieve the aims that you've set them, if you know what I mean. On the other hand I do believe that we are serving a public. Now if a public, who now have four governors, whereas the teachers only have two, if the public don't see eye to eye with the teachers on something you have the makings of a really big row, because both people have high expectations of success, if you know what I mean. The teachers expect their professionalism to be acknowledged and the parents will quite simply take their kids away. They're now in a position to send their kids to a school which suits the way they're organized. Now our local schools: Crouchlands, go in for quite a bit of streaming, Shortcross, who've been previously not massive rivals for us because they haven't got it together in academic terms particularly well, not that we have, but they are now marketing themselves much more and are talking about top ability sets and so on and quite honestly, if the English department don't give a good account of themselves to the parents, I'm afraid we will get people withdrawn.
>
> (Senior Deputy, Flightpath, 6 July 1989)

The relationship between 'the educational' and the market was also evident in a decision to group the new first year intake in such a way that the 28 'most able' students could be monitored (by a newly established Academic Attainment Monitoring Group, AAMG) and their performance enhanced if they appeared to be under-achieving. This was talked about in the following terms.

> I have to say though that our thinking about that was accelerated by the whole gathering realization that we were in the marketplace, and that having gone from a situation where we could rely upon being over-subscribed, we no longer could, and that there was a parental dimension to this which, if we didn't take notice of it, we'd die.
>
> (Senior Deputy, Flightpath, 6 July 1989)

The school has an average yearly intake of some 250 students and a drop in numbers for the 1991 intake had raised the issue of survival. The curriculum deputy indicated where they felt they might be losing out in the marketplace.

> But the call in October was, 'well let's really take this academic attainment thing seriously', because the parents we're losing are the aspiring middle class stereotypes, the caring parents those are the people who are asking questions like, how many people go to university, what are your results like as first questions, and those parents aren't that convinced of Flightpath. I think on the other side, we've got one of the largest SEN departments in the LEA. I think we can take the wheelchairs, the Misselthwaite pupils, and we can really develop there, we've raised questions about the level of homework in middle band, and the expectations of teachers.
>
> (Deputy Head, Flightpath, 6 July 1989)

As argued by the Conservative Government and market theorists one effect of competition and open enrolments is that schools will become far more sensitive to parental concerns and especially to academic performance. This is the mechanism that, it is argued, will produce rising standards. Clearly, the AAMG at Flightpath can be seen as evidence of how this might work. But it is not quite as simple as it seems. In part at least, the AAMG and grouping changes are part of a strategy intended to impress and attract different kinds of parents to the school. The aim is not so much to ensure greater 'value added' (as measured in terms of academic attainment) but to attract additional cultural capital into the school. Here we can see the possibility of a further elaboration of Bourdieu's metaphor (Bourdieu and Passeron 1977), schools are competing to attract greater cultural capital hoping for higher yielding returns. Students bearing solid cultural capital look like good longer-term investments. Like fund managers, headteachers can point to the returns from their portfolio in the hope of attracting more desirable clients. The question of who benefits and what is measured in all this becomes very confused.

EDUCATION, VALUES AND THE MARKET CULTURE

It is clear that the ideology and political rhetoric of the market, as directed towards the welfare state, celebrates the superiority of commercial planning and commercial purposes and forms of organization against those of public service and social welfare.

The argument is that the ends of public service will be achieved more effectively and efficiently by market means; although effectiveness and efficiency are often conveniently confused. Part of this shift from public service to competitive provision and client choice is achieved by legislative means (like changing the basis for school funding) but part of it also requires a change in culture and a change of values within the newly competitive educational enterprises. Keat (1991) makes precisely this point:

> During the course of the 1980s, the idea of an enterprise culture has emerged as a central motif in the political thought and practice of the Conservative government in Britain. Its radical programme of economic and institutional reform had earlier been couched primarily in the rediscovered language of economic liberalism, with its appeals to the efficiency of markets, the liberty of individuals and the non-interventionist state. But this programme has increasingly also come to be presented in 'cultural' terms, as concerned with the attitudes, values and forms of self-understanding embedded in both individual and institutional activities. Thus the project of economic reconstruction has apparently been supplemented by, or at least partly redefined as, one of cultural reconstruction – the attempt to transform Britain into an 'enterprise culture'.
>
> (p.1)

In part this will come about via the 'forced' adaptation of individuals and institutions to the new methods and constraints of the quasi-market – adjust and survive. Some schools, some teachers clearly embrace the new culture wholeheartedly and, in addition, new actors are arriving on the scene; governors from industry, consultants and bursars, bringing with them the new values and sometimes advocating 'new ways of thinking', new forms of self-understanding. But as we stressed in Chapter 1, educational reform involves complex processes of adaptation, mediation and resistance. Reform does not eliminate historical cultures, it confronts them. Concerns about values and ethics have surfaced regularly as the case study schools began to come to grips with the education market. Certain aspects of marketing and competition were reacted against, caused discomfort, stimulated debate. But then again others were taken up unproblematically and incorporated into 'normal' practice and 'normal' ways of thinking.

One point that was made time and time again in interviews and at meetings we observed was the danger of a wholesale transfer of commerical practices from industry into schools. Central here was the belief that the rhetoric of the market actually lacks subtlety. Most teachers are unhappy with the assumption that enrolling parents and educating students is exactly like marketing and producing baked beans! However we start not with a teacher but with an industrial governor from Pankhurst school, who is a senior manager from a large multinational company.

> There are two tasks which to my mind are perfectly prosaic really and low key, in terms of running a business, and that is, the first task is, as it were, getting the turnover up and in particular, the way that the LMS formula, budgeting formula works, is that it's in our interests to do so, as it is in any business. We've got two prongs to the marketing. One is that we go out and generate what the textbooks would say primary demand and the school, I would have to say, feels a bit edgy about that if what we are talking about is taking, is getting our entrants at the expense of other schools in the LEA, we feel a bit edgy about that, collectively. However, we feel less edgy about going outside the Borough, which of course is in our financial interest anyway, because such children come with more money with them. So there's a certain amount of edginess about doing the marketing in a sort of proper business, zero sum game sense. Then, second, is the question of massaging and currying favour and cosseting the parents of the children who have put their names down and there, we've got a much clearer conscience, as it were, and we've got one or two ideas about how to keep close to such families and of course it's a very delicate balance because there's no slack in the system.
>
> (8 February 1990)

In exploring the extent and nature of Pankhurst's market he makes two points about the ethics of educational markets. The first (above) relates to marketing and competing with other schools. Significantly he is unhappy about the idea of engaging in aggressive marketing *inside* Riverway LEA, but happy to try and attract students away from other LEAs' schools. The existing administrative 'boundaries' of the local state appear to engender some sense of mutual 'belonging' which raises ethical questions about open competition within the LEA. However, it could be argued that there is no logical reason, in 'pure' marketing terms, for seeing a difference between schools inside or outside a particular LEA. Indeed the Greenwich, Kingston and Bromley 'rulings' all seek to promote cross-borough competition between schools (TES 1991). What appears as a legal, technical and administrative matter is at root a matter of the politics of space (see earlier in this chapter). In effect the Act is trying to remove attachments to locality and deregulate space, in market terms. Such deregulation is clearly producing unease and outright resistance which may well result in changes in the nature of educational markets. This governor is less concerned about the 'cosseting' of parents who have already shown an interest in Pankhurst and is indicating the historical relationship with the private sector and the way some parents 'double-book' to ensure their child gets a place. This particular competitive relationship has been in operation for many years and its parameters are well understood. Significantly, the concern within the National Association of Headteachers about the ethics of marketing has led to the issuing of a code of practice. This code notes that: 'Many of those who work in schools worry that the pressure to market could lead to practices which do not match professional ethics. There is justification in this as some examples have already shown' (NAHT 1991, para. 3.7). The NAHT is clearly sceptical about the effects of an untrammelled market. It is suggested that: 'schools ought to consider very carefully the possibility of working as part of a group to develop the better aspects of marketing without creating some of the more damaging elements' (para. 3.9). And an unequivocal position is taken on the politics of space. 'Firstly, a school should direct its efforts to the immediate community which it serves', and, 'schools must be careful not to be seen to be adopting a deliberate policy of poaching' (para. 3.10). The document clearly aims at a compromise between public sector professionalism and cut-throat business competition. 'By stressing the individuality of the school rather than its superiority, members would enhance its image without entering into conflict with colleagues. Fair competition is acceptable, open conflict is not' (para. 5.3). But the second point (below) also made by the business governor from Pankhurst, comes in his response to the question of industrial sponsorship. Again he raises the ethical dimension and the possible limits that might need to be applied by schools.

> The ethics of raising funds, *per se*, I have no problem with, but then if you were to say tobacco companies and alcohol companies and so on, then I personally think that that is a personal issue rather than anything which is absolute. I mean I would be against having tobacco companies and alcohol companies sponsoring with their money. But there are, they get to very fuzzy boundaries. Companies that trade with South Africa, that sort of thing. But no, the fundamental idea of getting industrial business money in, I find no problem with at all.
>
> (8 February 1990)

In broad terms what he is reflecting upon is money and how far any institution might be willing to go to maximize its income. However, as we have already noted, Pankhurst school begins from a position of relative security. One of the deputies at Parkside, rather less optimistically, foresees possible situations in which the 'quantitative approach' and the 'financial' might begin to encroach upon the schools more idealistic concerns with the quality of education. Which should 'drive' the institution, which should determine its culture and values? (We pursue this further in Chapter 6).

> I think there's no doubt at all that the finance and the quantitative approach is very much in the picture. I've always tried to keep it no more than in the middle ground, I don't think that the school should be driven purely by finance. If the school has stable numbers or slightly increasing numbers, I can see that we can maintain that position, almost idealistic position, if you like. But I can see that once the school starts going into decline then it is finance which is going to determine the quality of the product. But while we're stable I'd like to see us maintaining the quality of education as opposed to quantity of education. But I think I can say that, as far as we're concerned, that it is the quality of education which has been the driving force so far, and then see if we've got enough money to deliver it.
>
> (Senior Deputy, Parkside, 26 March 1990)

The Senior Deputy at Flightpath makes a similar point but extends his concern to question the extent to which industrial models and educational principles can happily coexist in the school.

That is an obvious industrial model and you can quite easily make excuses along those lines, that you're going to develop the new building, which has to make money, and that is definitely a management decision, it's definitely a decision which takes, which involves the whole school, energies used and so on and so forth. And how fast schools can become income-generating institutions I'm still very unclear about. I mean, I can see that if you put someone like Terry in that position and briefed him to spend time he can earn his own salary and more, it's definitely possible. I can see that you can take on a massive undertaking like the sports hall, with some support from the LEA and make it work. All these things are possible, I see they're all possible. But what I'm concerned about is whether they are moving towards if you like, an industrial model for education, whether it stays within the bounds of what is the educational principles, aims and objectives of the school.

(28 November 1990)

What emerges here is a possible, instrinsic value conflict between business methods and education as a public service or, at the very least, business methods and the idea of a comprehensive education. This is further pointed up by the observations of one of the main grade teachers.

Well it is the market forces, which is in fact where I think again education is going to be hijacked, perhaps badly you know. As was said for example, in one of the videos we did see, as a sort of introduction to the National Curriculum. We are not like the marketplace, we can't change, we can't get rid of, what was the sort of phrase, unproductive sort of products, like certain pupils. We have to carry on and so on, and maybe evolve the situation which, we could perhaps make our pupils more productive. But how do you do that? Well I suppose the variety of ways for the future could be endless, like opting out or with greater selection procedures going on or in fact a kind of selling of the school to the feeder primary schools in a way that would try and get say the primary schools to feed particular kind of pupils into your school. And all these kind of ruses could be brought about, and that in fact makes education much more of a manipulative sort of thing in a way. And yes, there is the marketplace isn't there, operating very strongly, and yes, teachers are under pressure to produce. In the end of course, what may well become perhaps the whole reason for the exercise, these wonderful glowing exam results, at the end of the exercise, where you are in the pecking order, how your school fares. Because in the end, when the parents in fact of tomorrow or whatever, armed with the National Curriculum, and with various other sort of government information, are going to ask that sort of question, 'It's all very well your school having this wonderful building, as they do ask anyway, and these marvellous computers, but what are your exam results like?' And everything becomes very empirical in the end, doesn't it? It's all quantified to how many As and Bs and Cs you've got, and what staff are getting these and what staff are not and therefore of course if they're not, what can be done about it. So that at the end of the day we're marking schools as being a good school or a bad school, irrespective of what education is going on, is any good at all.

Part of the advocacy for the market in education as we have noted is based upon the argument that competition will raise 'standards'. One problem is of course that of defining standards, are they examination results and national test scores or other less easily quantifiable aspects of school life? Furthermore, what are the other possible consequences of parents using the cruder indicators to compare schools when making their choice of secondary schools? For this main grade teacher the market could 'enter' the educational process via parental demand for quantifiable standards (examination results) as ways of comparing schools. (Certainly this is one way that the ERA intends national testing to operate.) His own view of standards goes beyond examination results but in the nightmare scenario he paints he sees the forces of the market dictating the future of educational change. Results = standards = education = results. And there are other negative effects stemming from the market which were raised in interviews. In particular, senior teachers were becoming aware that the market and marketing brought with it new costs. The devolution of budgets and LMS had no provision for these new costs. Thus, the more time and resources devoted to market activities meant less time and resources available for direct educational activities.

As I said before, quality control is going to be essential, I think when you have a surplus of places, a surplus of schools in the local authority within an area, chasing pupils, that the competition between them is such that a great deal of time is going to be spent on promoting your institution as opposed to delivering the product within the school. It's got to be spent on showing outsiders what you do, much more than educating the children within it and I think that is a shame. I think if we were in the situation where we were all assured of our security, we would still give a high quality service, we wouldn't be distracted by seeing if we can survive.

(Senior Deputy, Parkside, 27 November 1989)

The Head of Overbury expressed very similar concerns:

There are some things which are not ideal about LMS, and they are bringing to bear pressures on schools which one would have hoped not to have had. One of the things I think is the whole thing of marketing which, if we are not careful, is going to become too sharp. As is the case of the school that was giving away 10 per cent reductions on showers. It seems to me that that is a kind of excess which one wants to avoid. But LMS is not just to deal with that, it's easy to quote these things and say well therefore LMS is ridiculous. A lot of LMS and the other new things really highlight the rather old-fashioned, rather inefficient, and in some cases, a bit slovenly ways in which many schools might have been run, ten or 20 years ago. I mean we should already have in schools what LMS is helping us to achieve. We should have very clear procedures for the disposal of money.

(15 January 1990)

In short, if managing educational expenditure 'efficiently' and being less 'slovenly' are seen as one positive result of LMS, linking it to the market has only added new, unwelcome pressures and given rise to new dilemmas. Is it ethical, in the new educational market, to portray or even imply that other schools are 'not as good' in any area of their educational provision? (Clearly, the NAHT believes that this is 'not on'.) The Senior Deputy at Parkside:

Schools which are successful in the early years of LMS, they are going to be shot at by other schools because it's the natural thing. Schools feel that they have a right to exist and that people have got their hearts and minds, entire careers tied up in institutions, which they deeply believe in, and they're not going to see it sink, and they're going to try to show it as better than the other places. Not necessarily a slightly different syllabus from the other places, recognizing that clients outside may prefer one sort of system to another one. And if we offer true opportunity to have different experiences in school, that's one thing, if we try to show that other schools in some way are not as good as us, I think that's detrimental to the cause of education generally and my worry is we shall spend so much time arguing and looking over our shoulders at what other people are doing and what other people are saying about us, that it may neglect what we're actually doing ourselves.

(27 November 1989)

Here the the market does not raise standards, it threatens them. It does not draw attention to the remediation of weaknesses, it encourages image-building and hype. It does not lead to productive self-evaluation but to an unhealthy concern with what the competition is offering, with mimicry, with faddish attention-seeking. The Head of Overbury was certainly unhappy about the way in which collaboration between schools was breaking down and earlier 'agreements' between schools were being 'reneged' upon in response to competitive pressures.

It is clear that people feel more strongly and are set more in competition with each other, for example, about curriculum issues, which may be leading to parents choosing one school as opposed to another. The broad and balanced science which was being discussed in the LEA, some schools are now offering only a single option of broad and balanced science, in order to be able to still offer languages or to be able to offer more English. And schools who originally felt that the whole LEA was committed to broad and balanced science, double broad and balanced science, 20 per cent broad and balanced science are actually, are feeling very, very angry now that people are not fulfilling obligations and they're withdrawing. Parents will now be able to drive a wedge and say well I'm going to that school now, I'm not coming to you because. . .

(15 January 1990)

The same sense of identification with local state boundaries is evident here as it was with the industrial governor we quoted earlier (co-operation within the LEA, competition with 'outsiders', i.e. the other LEAs). The market is seen to be destroying a beneficial educational collaboration. For marketers this would simply be the unacceptable face of the 'cartel' interfering with the operation of market forces. While for educators the chance to develop the curriculum and pedagogy in co-operation represents a genuine chance to ensure the spread of good practice. Two very different value systems are in confrontation here.

According to the market theorists the overall effect of market forces is the production of a new social order; institutional response is driven by choices made. And in this scenario the aggregate of consumer choices is always superior to professional judgement. The market is a mechanism, it is argued, without principles. Principles lead to partizanship and distortion. But what is suggested by the material presented here is a more complex and fuzzier situation. The market is not value-free, and as a mechanism it is also driven by choices made by producers. The workings of a quasi-market in education present a whole set of difficult ethical issues which must be confronted by senior teachers in schools. Professional judgement would seem to have a central place here. Furthermore, the unproblematic relationships between market forces and educational standards seem, in practice, far from clear cut. The market encourages schools to compete for 'certain sorts of students'. And market activities in certain respects detract from educational ones. The insertion of quasi-market forces into education is a massive piece of social experimentation which is already generating a whole range of unanticipated consequences.

Chapter 3

LMS (the Local Management of Schools)and the entrepreneurial school

INTRODUCTION

In Chapter 4, on the National Curriculum, we will look at policy as an ongoing process and will suggest that it is helpful to see it as multifaceted, with interrelated policy arenas each containing the facets of intended policy, actual policy and policy-in-use. In the case of LMS we begin by trying to clarify the Government's policy intentions, with regard to schools as institutions. This is a necessary forerunner because the legislation itself, the actual policy, is written in a technical–bureaucratic language that does not make clear the underlying intentions of LMS. We then go on to explore the micro-political dimension, i.e. the way in which Government policy, in all its complexity, finds a presence within one school. The purpose is to try and grasp both the extent and the way in which LMS has entered the discourses of schooling and how the institutional practices may be changing as a consequence. This provides us with a series of questions.

What does the ERA, market-based view of education actually involve and how does the Government intend to make the 'connection' between the market and the institutional practices of the schools? How, in crude terms, is the climate set by the market intended to affect the micro-climate of the schools? This leads us to ask how the Act in general and LMS in particular, anticipate a new culture of management within 'schools as enterprises' and how the new institutional practices of schooling are intended to change the relationships between schools and the State (local and national), parents, governors and employers?

LMS AND THE SCHOOL AS AN ENTERPRISE

Unlike the development of the National Curriculum, LMS has no roots in the educational world. Its ideological genealogy derives, partly, from nineteenth century laissez-faire politics and the more recent writings of neo-liberal economists such as Hayek (1976) and Friedman (1980), and partly from more recent developments in organizational theory (Caldwell and Spinks, 1988, pp. 3–25). To this extent it is not directly concerned with matters of pedagogy, theories of learning or questions about assessment. Rather, LMS reflects a strand in Tory thinking that wishes to alter significantly the relationship between the State, social policy provision and institutional management. Put simply, it seeks to privilege 'market mechanisms' over and above a State co-ordinated and managed system.

For neo-liberals, such as Hayek and Friedman, the market solution to the planning and delivery of education rests on two premises. Firstly the belief that decentralized markets maximize creative entrepreneurship through the drive for profit, and are thus better for coping with rapid social and technological change and with uncertainty:

> Through the pursuit of selfish aims the individual will usually lead himself to serve the general interest, the collective actions of organized groups are almost invariably contrary to the general interest. (Hayek 1976, p.138)

This may not produce equality, indeed that would be counter-productive in market terms, but it is not seen to be unfair. Thus the market will provide a natural economic order and even the poorest should benefit from the progress of the society as a whole. Secondly, freedom of choice can only be fully achieved in the marketplace, as against the coercion of monopolistic state provision. The imposition of taxation to fund state provision is unfavourably contrasted with the opportunity to dispose of one's own income:

> An essential part of economic freedom is freedom to choose how to use our income; how much to spend on ourselves and on what items . . . we choose in the light of our own needs and desires.
>
> (Friedman 1980, p.89)

The Education Reform Act 1988 realizes these central premises by seeking to establish the mechanisms and conditions for a market in education (see Ball 1990a). Its operation is to rest on five main, interrelated factors:

- *Choice* via 'open enrolment';
- *Diversity* via the extension of the current choice of schools;
- *Competition* via the diversity of schools competing to be 'chosen' by parents, thus moving control of education away from the producers (teachers) and towards the consumers ('parents, pupils, the local community and employers');
- Per capita *funding* to connect the 'product' to market forces, with individual school funding being primarily determined by student numbers (each student enrolled bringing a fixed sum to the school enabling parental views of the comparative performances of different schools to have direct financial consequences);
- *Organization* requiring schools to take direct control of their individual budgets, thus linking the new funding system to the internal school decision-making, that is by connecting the management of the school directly to market forces.

The key question posed for schools by the Act is not simply how cost-effective is the running of the school but, how cost effectively are you processing students in line with the National Curriculum? Schools are encouraged to balance their budgets and generate the maximum income to enhance the product. The educational process becomes the production process, teachers are producers, parents are consumers, knowledge becomes a commodity and the educated student the product, with a minimum specification laid down by the National Curriculum. It is further asserted that a budget-conscious system of organizational decision-making will raise educational standards. Under LMS it is hoped this process, operating at an institutional level, will be driven by the educational market which effectively charges the schools with 'managing their own salvation'. Thus the Government's ideological commitment to market forces is combined with a critique of existing institutional practices in a way that privileges organizational and managerial concerns. It is not simply a matter of 'linking' the market to individual schools but of setting out to transform institutional forms of educational provision, in particular the notion of a State 'system'. Briefly, there is, in New Right thinking, a strong belief that a State-run educational system produces systemic dependency (schools dependent upon 'the system'), complacency (an unresponsiveness to the demands of society), bureaucracy (initiatives for change hampered by 'red tape') and 'protectionism' (educational quality judged by the 'professionals', whose central concerns may not be in the national or the consumers' interests). The argument then follows that such tendencies can only be eradicated if spending is devolved to schools as individual enterprises required to respond to some form of educational market. For the Government, the essence of LMS is buried within the move to market-driven funding. This encourages schools to enter a new era of self-help, entrepreneurialism, cost-effectiveness and consumerism.

Self-determination

The promotion of self-determination is intended to erode any sense of an educational 'system' and replace it with a market-driven, free-floating, diverse set of enterprises (schools), charged with delivering products (schooled persons) with a minimum quality specification (the skills and knowledge of the National Curriculum). The management of change is to rest with the schools, diminishing any sense of dependency upon the State or 'the system' and heightening the need for entrepreneurialism.

Entrepreneurialism

This is seen to follow as part of the new management culture of the 'school as enterprise', that is a releasing of the entrepreneurial skills of individuals within the organization and the use of more 'effective' management models from the business world. (Goodchild and Holly 1989; Keep 1990).

Cost-effectiveness

Cost-effectiveness in providing the service will be achieved by driving out the inefficiencies of 'the system', the bureaucratic inertia and the 'Town Hall politics' by devolving decisions to the schools.

Consumerism

Finally, 'consumerism' will privilege parents and employers in judging the quality of the education provided and reduce what is seen as the self-interested power of the producer lobby, i.e. the educationalists.

The Government wants to move towards an educational service that is differently provided and managed, in which high choice and diversity will create the basis for a new relationship within schools, between schools and around schools. In the 'natural environment' of the market, free from the 'contamination' of a system, schools should release the 'natural' gifts of individuals; enterprise, initiative and the instinct for survival. The 'successful' schools will be those that become self-determining enterprises, promoting innovative and cost-effective approaches to fulfilling consumer demand. Removing the constraints of the system will allow the schools to 'do what should come naturally' (Keat and Abercrombie 1991). We can sum this up in Figure 3.1.

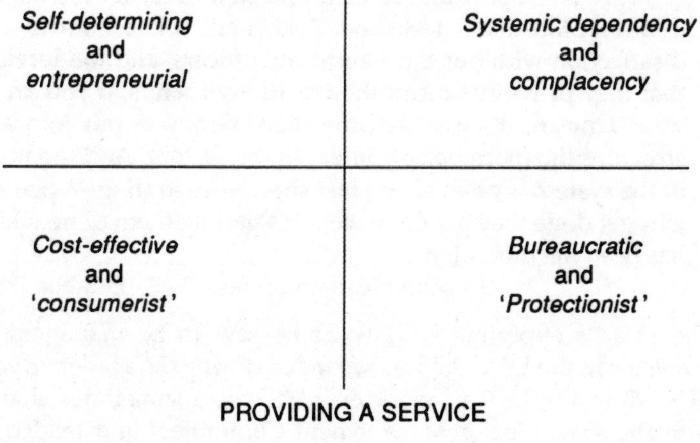

| MARKET DRIVEN
HIGH
'CHOICE/DIVERSITY' | vs. | STATE SYSTEM
LOW
'CHOICE/DIVERSITY' |

MANAGING CHANGE

| *Self-determining*
and
entrepreneurial | *Systemic dependency*
and
complacency |
| *Cost-effective*
and
'consumerist' | *Bureaucratic*
and
'Protectionist' |

PROVIDING A SERVICE

Figure 3.1 Market and state provision of education.

We move on to present a school, referred to here as Flightpath School, in which there is a degree of willingness to move towards the new ERA, but where changing the institutional practices is proving a formidable challenge. We argue here that the move from state provision to 'individualist', market-driven enterprises may well produce changes within schools that for the Government are both unanticipated and unwelcome.

LOCAL MANAGEMENT IN ACTION

Going it alone

Transforming the 'old' into the 'new' revolves around freeing schools from the 'dead hand' of the LEAs and allowing them to decide, for themselves, how to spend the 'housekeeping money'. Within Flightpath Comprehensive the early perception among many senior staff, and the Head in particular, was that LMS genuinely offered an opportunity for schools to 'do their own thing' and break free from the financial and administrative constraints of the past, to become *self-determining*. In general terms, the constraints from the LEA were less to do with matters of policy and more to do with perceived 'inefficiencies' in the system.

> But I do believe firmly that schools often would be better managers of themselves, if they had more direct managerial control over finance and staffing and all the rest of it, so there's a lot of LMS that I welcome. And that's related not to any disaffection with our local authority officers, and the services that they provide. I mean they're all my friends, if you know what I mean, it's just that the more tiers you put into any structure the more noise you get in the system. And the noise in the system is often sheer, just sheerly frustrating. When the jobs get done they get done well. It's getting them done which has been the difficulty.
>
> (Deputy Head, interview, 28 September 1989)

The Head's experiences of what he saw to be management problems in the LEA, (he was seconded during the academic year 1989/90 to the LEA to work on LMS) were sometimes shared with the SMC (Senior Management Committee) and tended to confirm people's suspicion that the LEA was occasionally unsure in its sense of direction and sometimes inefficient in carrying out its tasks. 'Going it alone' was increasingly seen as an opportunity to provide education more efficiently and effectively.

The school's firm belief in its own capacity to manage change helped to produce an enthusiasm to get to grips with LMS. Not just to start spending the money more wisely than the LEA, which was taken to be almost axiomatic among the SMC, but also to start managing in a more entrepreneurial, cost-effective and consumerist way. Early LMS training encouraged this and, after one training session, the Head asked one of the deputies to comment to the SMC on his view of the day:

> One thing to say is that it is nowhere near as frightening as people have given us to believe, as long as we are logical and sensible.
>
> (Deputy, SMC, 21 September 1989)

This confidence partly reflects the history of a school in which good management has been considered an important feature of school life. The Head has paid great attention to 'honing' the management structure and defining the job specifications of the senior managers. These skills of school management were seen as transferrable to managing 'the enterprise'; the rational and logical application of higher managerial skills were taken to be a necessary and sufficient basis for tackling the problems of institutional change. However, what was unclear was the extent to which models from the private business sector were applicable in the school (Keep 1990) and there were fears about some of these models:

> At the moment there are a lot of cowboys, yuppie personnel, who are talking in terms of performance indicators as if they rule the world, and I'd only liken it to people who believe that the free enterprise economy is infallible. It isn't, and performance indicators can do as much damage as they can do benefit, if they are not sensibly determined and operated. And the thing that worries me is the combination of financial theories overriding educational philosophies combined with cost-cutting enterprises, using a criteria of performance as a cutting edge.
>
> (Deputy Head, interview, 28 September 1989)

This unease has been alluded to elsewhere (Bowe and Ball 1990) and it is becoming increasingly clear that applying the principles of LMS to the development of school managerial systems is by no means straightforward. For instance, at Flightpath the Head was keen on devolving the INSET budget to departments, seeing it as a logical development from LMS, and a 'liberating idea':

> 'It is a sort of LMS for the departments' (Head). However, such a view was not embraced by one of the Senior Teachers who was concerned that deciding who was entitled to INSET was not in the hands of the Heads of Department (HODs), and it was therefore unfair to make them pay out of their budget. The Head then suggested that calculations could be made to compensate for the departmental differences in control over their budgets.
>
> (Observation notes, SMC, 18 January 1990)

Here there is an important difference between devolved budgeting and the making of financial policy. Who is to be involved in institutional policy-making, and how, cannot be 'read-off' from the 1988 Act and, in practice, accommodating to the demands of the Act *in toto* has tended to mean that decision-making increasingly rests with a small group of staff (Bowe and Ball 1990), pulling schools away from the new management styles of 'post-Fordism' and back towards technocratic, hierarchical managerial styles:

> I mean you cannot expect the classroom teacher, as we have in this school, a relatively young, inexperienced staff, to understand the finances of the school. There is this polarization where your classroom teacher will concentrate on obviously trying to achieve the National Curriculum, where the management, whilst very much aware of the National Curriculum, and what staff are trying to do, has also to balance the books on LMS. And certainly I would suggest that for the very senior managers in the school, the Head, the First Deputy, the Bursar, their minds have been concentrated very much on LMS during the last few months.
>
> (Senior teacher, interview, 23 March 1990)

Whether the school will begin to evolve more democratic and participatory management remains to be seen. However, the impact of LMS on many non-senior teachers has been to enhance their sense of exclusion from their working situation. In this sense the notion of self-determination only applies to a rather small section of the school's teachers.

Furthermore, a tension between the push for decentralization and devolution and the continued concern for technical–scientific rationality and control is clearly evident (Harvey 1990). This is more than a symptom of a transitionary phase, a temporary feature in which authority is used to develop ultimate freedoms. 'Self-determining' schools remain nested within a social world in which aspects of the 'self' (in institutional and individual terms) are partly determined elsewhere. For example, in Flightpath there has been a growing awareness that a major part of the budget will not be determined by the school, as the Head made clear at a meeting of the middle/junior management:

> I'm sure all this is the same for a lot of other schools and shouldn't we just decide upon the needs and be prepared to overspend.
>
> (Head of third year)

> But that's the unreal world and it's not negotiable and you might as well accept that . . . I can assure you that there'll be no expansion in Westway and I could take you through the detailed economics of the formula and the rest. We've got high idealism and we'd need higher resources than we've got. It's as straightforward as that.
>
> (Head)

He then gave an example:

> If it means you have to change your methods then that's what you'll have to do. I mean chalk and talk is cheaper than a sort of individualized carousel and we'll just have to make those choices.
>
> (Head, Curriculum Council meeting, 5 March 1990)

Here financial self-determination appears to translate into financial constraint. Thus financial arguments for educational change are set *against* the professional judgements of teachers. It is hard to see this as either an indicator of greater efficiency or as a mechanism for raising standards, *unless* one accepts a priori that the teachers' judgements are always unsound. If one adds to this the need to respond to the externally imposed demands of the National Curriculum then it is difficult to see the majority of teachers feeling any sense of self-determination. The dilemma is apparent in this comment from one of the deputy heads:

> I'd love to think LMS would solve that, but I can't see it. Under LMS we have formula funding with laws laid down from the outside and the bottom line is that group sizes may have to go up to get the flexibility we need to deliver the curriculum experiences we want to deliver.
>
> (Senior Deputy, SMC, 8 March 1990)

Consequently we need to recognize that the possibilities for autonomous self-management are powerfully circumscribed by aspects of the budget over which schools may have little or no control. For example, those parts of the budget made up by (a) the level of LEA expenditure (increasingly determined by the politics of local taxation), (b) the allocation via the 'formula' to each school (which has its own particular politics), and (c) the vagaries of the local, micro-educational markets (the levels of finance in bordering LEAs and the inherited pupil numbers and state of the 'plant' in neighbouring schools), as well as the potential for parental and employer sponsorship (thus raising the question of whether the new conditions of schooling allow all schools an equal opportunity to succeed).

Further, it is precisely the uncertainties introduced by this lack of autonomy that produces a sense of continual information deficit, ironically a situation the SMC finds itself trying to resolve through 'tighter' administration and the active management of change. Thus devolution of management need not equal a devolution of power. As Ainley has suggested, LMS is in part an attempt by the Government to privatize the problems of financing schools (Ainley 1990). Thus while self-determination appears to provide schools with new freedoms, it also opens them up to blame for their 'failures' and leaves them with the dilemmas and contradictions inherent in government policy, a policy they had little opportunity to 'determine'.

Being entrepreneurial

One way in which the Government is suggesting schools increase their level of self-determination is by making themselves far less dependent upon the state for all their finances. The 'added extra' which might provide greater budget flexibility could be found through a more *enterpreneurial* approach. This notion of enterprise in LMS refers to both the school as an organization and to the people that work within it (Keat and Abercrombie 1991). The Government hope schools will show enterprise by taking risks and being innovative in a commercial sense by modelling themselves on commercial enterprises, franchised to deliver the National Curriculum. They also hope this new culture and philosophy of the 'school as enterprise' will release the entrepreneurial skills of individuals within the organization. Wrapped up in the Government's appeal for greater self-determination is the image of the macho world of the self-made man [sic]; the individual whose drive, flair and initiative seizes the present and builds the future. The new culture of enterprise in schools will produce better management (of money and people) and the generation of new sources of income.

Within Flightpath making the connections between financial concerns and educational concerns has not been straightforward. The major device has been the School Management Plan which has dominated the work of the SMC for much of the year. Throughout that time there were frequent pleas from the senior managers for more time to 'ensure that the basics were still being done'; that matters of discipline, dealing with 'cover' and supply and pastoral work should not be neglected while trying to put together a management plan for the school. Being 'entrepreneurial' requires *time* to project likely income, to pursue additional income and to decide how this will be spent by somehow bringing educational aims and financial calculations into line. Finding that time has caused considerable problems:

> There is a tendency to say, look, this is where the buck stops, finance-wise, if you haven't got the money you can't do it, but not to apply the same sort of stringency when you're talking about staff time and resources. We've only got a limited amount of staff time resources, we can't handle this, this is where it stops ... bang.
>
> (Senior Deputy, interview, 16 January 1990)

The outcome has been incredible pressure on senior staff to 'deliver' a new, entrepreneurial management thrust while trying to keep hold of the educational issues that 'won't go away'.

Furthermore getting a clear picture of future income has been no easy matter:

In purely financial terms we ought to know the missing links in a year's time, therefore we ought to have that final certainty, we ought to have that final clarity. I think what will then happen is that the certainty will may be dictate to us, small though resources are, what we have relative to what we put into our management plan, and we might then say that we've in fact not prioritized. You see that's another thing, we've drawn up priorities in the SMP but against what? We don't know, and so it might well be that we've been hopelessly optimistic about our resources.

(Senior Deputy, interview, 16 January 1990)

Innovation, risk and enterprise tend to flourish in a context where the risks can be calculated, income can be calculated and the consequences of failure are acceptable. In these respects the conditions at Flightpath are not particularly favourable. Despite this they have 'taken a risk' with a new sports hall, jointly funded by the LEA and a loan to the school. The long-term problem will be the servicing of the debt. Already the need to repay parts of the loan before the hall starts to earn significant amounts of money from outside is giving cause for concern:

The burden of the sports hall means we really do need a generous local benefactor to see us through.

(Head, SMC, 29 January 1990)

More recently the Head has observed:

There's not the money available in industry that there was and it's now got to the point where the time spent chasing it may be too much.

(Head, SMC, 14 May 1990)

It remains to be seen how much impact the funding of a debt will have upon the educational processes of the school in the next few years. But in taking on this new responsibility the school has become tangled up in the leisure and financial markets; both notoriously unstable in the last few years. Educational survival may now be open to the fluctuations of markets over which the school will have little control; potentially eroding further the sense of self-determination as the school tries to respond to a variety of very different markets. Thus, for Flightpath, self-determination and market-driven funding may come to stand in stark opposition to one another. It is indeed sobering to note that the 'Thatcherite' dream of economic revival based upon flourishing small businesses has actually produced a high number of failures and casualties in the small business sector of the economy.

At the individual level of enterprise Flightpath promoted a member of staff to the position of marketing manager, in September 1989, although he retains responsibility for IT in the school and is therefore limited in the time he has to pursue his marketing role. Nonetheless in the SMC meetings at the end of 1989 questions of marketing and seeking funds externally became so frequent the following appears in the observation notes:

> *Note*: Conversation with Senior Deputy re the appearance of 'marketing' as a vital sub-text of the meeting. He feels the establishment of the marketing group and the appointment of a marketing manager has been important here.
>
> (Observation notes, SMC, 2 October 1989)

Although 'raising people's consciousness' of marketing has had an impact upon their way of seeing educational issues it does not mean the contradictions between educational and marketing issues are any easier to resolve. The major financial success of the marketing manager has been to secure a suite of computers by getting a computer firm to use the school's name in a national advertising campaign. While this will undoubtedly provide short-term flexibility elsewhere in the budget such sources of funding do tend to come in the form of 'one-off' deals. They cannot provide for long-term stability, predictability or continuity in the level of funding. Long-term planning may therefore become difficult and increasingly limited to the 'known' aspects of funding, thus in effect restraining the sought-after flexibility.

Getting value for money

The other side of the planning coin relates to expenditure. The government intends LMS to encourage schools to be *cost-effective*. Interestingly effectiveness and efficiency as conceptions for planning are confused and welded together in such a notion. Deciding the cost of books, laboratory equipment or paper has never been a difficult task. Neither is it an insurmountable problem to locate or monitor overall staff costs or the cost of repair work on the school:

These figures are illustrative of those that have been submitted to the DES. If we have to have a 4 per cent cut in our budget, if we have to shed £70,000 and staff are 80 per cent of our budget it's tempting to cut 4.5 per cent of our staff. However, we could do it in other ways and therefore we do have to cost all the elements and that includes time. Time now costs money and we mustn't forget that.

(Head, SMC, 30 October 1989)

The real difficulty lies in calculating the cost of 'activities', particularly teaching activities and then setting these against marketing or fund-raising. This is made even more problematic by the need to calculate the effectiveness of any activity. This is well illustrated in the next quote from observation notes:

They talked about the use of spare capacity at Flightpath, i.e. the home economics room, the sports hall, etc. These are not in constant use and could be used by some of the primary schools from time to time.

Perhaps we should pursue this and shouldn't charge them as a gesture of goodwill and as a good marketing strategy.

(Senior teacher)

Yes, I'd go along with that and we should look at it as a more cost-effective way of using our resources.

(Head, SMC, 8 February 1990)

Increasing the budget was set aside in order to market the school and its facilities and this was seen to be cost-effective. But there was no attempt in this instance to quantify the various elements and while the rhetoric was present the cost-benefit analysis was not. There has been frequent mention of the idea of an educational audit and some discussion of how the heads of department might be key figures in this process, but again finding time to do the calculations is not easy. Furthermore it is not certain that the skills necessary for such an audit are present within the school.

In a number of instances it appeared as if delegating the consequences of financial constraint assumed more importance than discussing the principles on which costs might be balanced with benefits.

For example, there was then an exchange over the question of budget accountability and the matter of the cost of field courses was raised, in particular biology and geography.

> It's very easy for people to say we'll do this course because someone else is picking up the bill. If we were to make it part of their departmental budget then they'd have to think about it, it would be helping people to become more aware of the cost of running their departments.
>
> (Head)

He then went on to suggest that the music department ought to have piano-tuning as part of their budget.

> Then they might choose to have only five pianos tuned each year instead of six. But it would be their choice.
>
> (Head)

One of the senior teachers was concerned that losing the field trips might seriously harm the marketing potential of the sixth form:

> I mean if we're trying to attract kids back into the sixth form with interesting courses . . .
>
> (Senior teacher)

Controlling expenditure was brought back into the argument by another of the senior teachers and the Head raised the matter of administrative efficiency:

> The advantage of keeping finance centralized is that I can negotiate the amount needed and not just allocate a fixed sum. People will always make sure they spend that fixed sum, even if they didn't need it.
>
> (Senior teacher)

> Yes, and you can also save money on some of the costs and make sure that National Insurance and all the paperwork we need to ensure is done, gets done.
>
> (Head)

The educational concern of the first senior teacher was reasserted.

> By delegating you might end up with them being axed, in the long term. I'm a very firm believer in residential trips in educational terms. Have we thought about the possibility of some sort of sponsorship?
>
> (Senior teacher)

In this exchange cost-effectiveness is tangled up with educational concerns, consumerism and self-determination. Interestingly the issue remains unresolved and this may well reflect the contradictory nature of working with LMS, which presents schools with precisely the dilemmas that successive governments have failed to resolve. This is also apparent in the next quotations:

> The risk here is that if you devolve too much you generate more bureaucracy with all the different budgets.
>
> (Head)

> If you devolve everything too far then you don't become cost-effective.
>
> (Senior teacher Observation notes, SMC, 14 May 1990)

This opens up the whole question of centralization vs. devolution, but in a micro-situation. We see here some of the same sort of solutions offered by members of the SMC as those suggested by politicians and social theorists for the State! 'Problems' for the management might be 'privatized' by getting other devolved budget holders to sort them out themselves (Ainley 1990). (A cynical view might be that this is a way of passing on cost-cutting decisions to others. Self-determination is reduced to choices between alternative expenditures.)

Keeping the customers satisfied

Finally, in developing some criteria for cost-effectiveness the Act encourages schools to be aware of the consumers. There is evidence that in general terms the Head and a number of the senior management team embrace the notion of *consumerism*.

> What the client group want is very important and I applaud the prospective parents' questionnaire, but we really need to go further on this.
>
> (Head, SMC, 30 October 1989)

> Question of teaching the sixth form for a longer period at exam time was raised, because other schools were doing so and some parents had expressed concern. It was decided to look at this.
>
> (Observation notes, SMC, 8 February 1990)

But this is not a new phenomenon at Flightpath.

Well, those of us that have been in Flightpath school a long time, have been concerned about our image since 1968. When I came here in '68, the school was considered one of the worst schools in the Borough, both in terms of its pupil behaviour, its levels of attainment, its buildings. So since 1968 through various managers and through all the staff, including the help from parents, we have been constantly trying to improve the image of the school. Both from a visual point of view the introduction of school uniform, which didn't exist in '68 in any form in the boys' school, through to raising the academic standards of the school. So we've been constantly working at that, and whilst one thinks that this is a new concept of marketing the school, it isn't.

(Deputy, interview, 28 September 1989)

In the above quotation the consumers are defined in terms of the parents and the community. But students are also consumers and have to be attracted to the school and retained. The difficulty that emerges then is not just deciding who the customer actually is, parents, employers or students or all of these, but which should have priority at any one time. In terms of entry to the school parents may be central, but then there is the question of retaining the commitment and involvement of the parents and the students, over time. Providing a 'student-friendly' school with an enjoyable and well received curriculum, may not be the same as ensuring future parents will choose the school. Also what of employers who may find the traditional nature of the National Curriculum unacceptable, how will they respond to requests for additional funding or for assistance on governing bodies? One 'solution' to this problem is offered in the Act which accords parents and employers greater privileges than the students, who are not statutorily required to be represented on the governing body, nor necessarily paramount in deciding which schools they go to. Far from being student-centred the Act actually 'positions' students in the traditionally dependent learner role, the *real* consumers are parents and employers. This places key aspects of the teachers' self-determination under threat:

For example, whilst this might be the ideal curriculum situation from their point of view, the realities are that we do have to provide an image to fulfil the requirement of the governors and the parents and I think one of the hardest areas that staff are trying to come to grips with at the moment is the reality that the governors and especially the parents, have a far greater say and influence in what goes on in the school, than they've ever experienced in the past.

(Senior teacher, interview, 23 March 1990)

The SMC has been very aware of the extent to which 'image' and attracting the parents can present difficulties in meeting the individual needs of the students. Again we have the multiple account of the 'customer', do you meet community needs (the image parents want) or the needs of the individual students? Such questions are profoundly distorted by the introduction of differences in student worth:

You are caught, and this is where LMS really raises its ugly head, in terms of true educational things. Each child has a price tag on it, and the sixth formers have the highest price tag, so in pure financial terms one obviously is trying to raise the most amount of money you can. But Flightpath staff have always been conscious of our intake being skewed towards the less able child, and through the years we have developed what has got to be considered one of the best supportive education departments in the Borough. But of course the less able children tend not to stay on to the sixth form, unless we feel they are really going to benefit from it, and we have an excellent record, through our guidance department of ensuring that our children get into employment as well. So you have this conflict of trying to ensure you've got a big sixth form, trying to ensure that you are really doing the best for the individual child, and the introduction of the disabled children. I don't think that's a sort of problem for us in terms of whether it was a bad image or not. I mean I think personally it can do nothing but good for us but one has got to recognize the fact that these children do take a lot of extra time.

(Senior teacher, interview, 23 March 1990)

Ironically, as Alder and Raab (1988) have pointed out, there is an interesting contradiction between increasing student numbers to gain greater income and the 'effectiveness' of the school. This may in turn have an impact on consumer demand. Consequently, if the DES insist upon the 1979 figures (though we have evidence that some LEAs are successfully circumventing these figures) the size of the school may actually count against the school, in the long term:

> One of the most off-putting things that we've had to overcome in this school, is the size of the school, 'cos when I came here, we were a 12-form entry, over 2,000 children, over 120 odd teaching staff, and parents coming from small primary schools, and if they were the quieter, meeker children, were very intimidated. So we've had to work very hard at proving to them that big did not necessarily mean ugly and uncontrollable.
>
> (Senior teacher, interview, 23 March 1990)

SUMMARY

The new educational world of self-determining schools, disciplined by the market, is intended to produce a social order in which the 'natural' talents and inclinations of individuals and organizations can come to the fore. However, our research suggests that far from releasing people from the burdens of bureaucracy LMS may well increase the internal administrative load. In addition 'being enterprising' requires risk capital and time. In the case study reported here, the former has been raised partly out of the 'system', but also via a loan at the unknown cost of linking the school's finance to the presently depressed leisure and financial markets. Responding to the consumers brings difficulties in tying together the competing concerns of parents, employers and students.

The picture is not one of new freedoms. Rather the new elements introduced by LMS require schools to deal with a different, expanded and contradictory sets of demands. In trying to adjust to these demands schools are finding the new era, constructed by others on the basis of neo-liberal and management theories, massively pressured and often a distraction from the world of educating students. Important issues about the purposes of schooling in our society are being thrown up by the implementation of LMS, but they are not being addressed in public debate. The assumption of the superiority of the market appears unassailable. But perhaps we can leave the last word to the Senior Deputy at Flightpath:

If you just take the sports hall. You've had two out of four deputy heads intimately involved in setting it up, one from the resourcing point of view, one from the business management point of view. We had one senior teacher who is also very much involved in the nuts and bolts of it. You've got those three working all hours, those three really working early in the morning for the last six months. It's a huge soaking up of energy and somebody somewhere along the line has to evaluate that and say, 'is that part of the global target of the school?'

(Senior Deputy, interview, 28 November 1990)

Chapter 4

The National Curriculum: subject to change?

INTRODUCTION

Sociological discussion about the National Curriculum has been somewhat dominated by the tendency to see it fairly unproblematically as yet another example of the increasing State control of education (see Chapter 1). In researching the impact of the National Curriculum upon departmental policy the State control perspective can lead to the assumption that what we are looking at is an unproblematical 'implementation' of the National Curriculum in schools, an assumption that has been actively encouraged by the Government. (See for example, *National Curriculum: From Policy to Practice*, DES, 1989a, especially section 9.) Implicit here is the idea that we can read into the National Curriculum policy an unequivocal governmental position that will filter down through the quasi-state bodies (the NCC (National Curriculum Council) and the subject working parties) and into the schools. (The local authorities remain in a marginal position but are essentially seen to be supporting schools in their endeavours, helping schools to 'get change right')

However, as we have argued in Chapter 1, the National Curriculum policy process is a good deal more complex than this, requiring us to recognize there is a *dialectical process* in which the 'moments' of legislation (the Act), documentation (from the NCC, the DES, etc.), and 'implementation' (the work of the teachers) may be more or less loosely coupled. Policy texts are not closed, their meanings are neither fixed nor clear, and the 'carry over' of meanings from one policy arena and one educational site to another is subject to interpretational slippage and contestation. These texts are part of a continuous *policy cycle* consisting of significantly different arenas and sites within which a variety of interests are at stake. We shall go on to argue that while it is the case that the ERA *as a whole* aims to intervene in the workings of these arenas and sites in order to create a qualitatively different cycle with new conditions 'empowering' some at the expense of others, the different parts of the ERA may well be taken up differently by particular LEAs, schools and departments within schools, thus producing very different outcomes that may actually work against a *National* Curriculum. In other words, existing diversity in the educational system may well be exacerbated by the provisions of the ERA. In effect, the capacity of the State to successfully 'implement' a National Curriculum may in fact be limited and circumscribed by other aspects of the Act. While this may well appeal to those neo-liberals in the Tory party who have expressed concern about the whole principle of a National Curriculum, our research suggests that the present developments are not resulting in a curricular provision that is driven by 'the market', but a provision that is driven by serendipity, ad hockery, chaos and the minimum planning that such circumstances allow. The cost of all this within schools is measured by teachers' stress, resentment, illness, absenteeism and the number of those leaving the profession.

The notion of a continuous policy cycle draws attention specifically towards the work of policy recontextualization that goes on in the schools. Researching the school setting most certainly involves a careful consideration of the National Curriculum alongside the various elements that make up the Act, LMS Open Enrolment, opting out, etc., and the ways in which these empower different bodies, groups and individuals in different ways. But it also requires an investigation of the impact of matters of contingency – staff absence or shortage, individual personalities or capacities, the geographical location and demographic shifts in the catchment area, for example.

At the end of Chapter 1 we suggested that the primary policy contexts may provide what might be termed 'space for manoeuvre' throughout the policy cycle. Research will need to identify the nature and extent of resistance, accommodation, subterfuge and conformity within schools and between departments. Furthermore departmental work on the National Curriculum will be 'nested' within the LEA and school environments, albeit changing environments, that reflect the ways in which schools and authorities are adjusting to the new ERA *in toto*. These over-lapping environments provide a context in which the teaching resources, the policies and the ethos of the schools, the views of teachers, the levels of parental accountability and inspectorial checks, and responses to market forces may well fracture and diversify the 'implementation process' rather than encourage similarity and unity between schools. We are therefore sug-gesting that the complexity and interrelated nature of the various aspects of change may well confound a model of change that assumes a simplicity of process and a certain discreteness between the various elements of change.

We will present a sample of data from the four case-study schools. Most of these data are drawn from repeat interviews with heads of department, although others are quoted and some observation data are also included. The subjects referred to here are science, mathematics and English. The conclusions from the data are often quoted in general terms and all indications are that the sorts of issues raised here are to be found within virtually all schools involved in National Curriculum changes. Basically we want to convey something of the complexity of these changes.

We begin with the issue of interpretation, the 'reading' of policy texts, and go on to point out that such interpretations are not unconstrained, they do not develop in a vacuum and a variety of exigencies impinge upon the processes of interpretation. Thus we have two, interrelated, central concerns. One to explore the actual engagement of departments with the policy *texts* and the other to explore the engagement with and responses to the con-straints and possibilities arising within the changing *contexts* within which the departments operate. It is our contention that it is in the micro-political processes of the schools that we begin to see not only the limitations and possibilities State policy places upon schools but, equally, the limits and possibilities practi-tioners place upon the capacity of the State to reach into the daily lives of the schools.

INTERPRETING THE TEXTS

Departments and the whole curriculum?

Although the Government has laid out an overall structure for the National Curriculum, the setting down of the content and the skills to be taught in the individual subject areas and the cross-curricular themes and dimensions is actually being undertaken and introduced into schools in a piecemeal fashion. In our research schools the relationship between subject departments and the full curriculum of the school has varied, although all the schools have had a strong subject-based departmental bias. Up to now such a basis for organizing the curriculum has only gradually been eroded by fairly limited cross-curricular concerns, for example personal and social education or topic-based work. The impetus for departments to 'look outwards' and develop cross-curricular links has tended to come from senior teachers, curriculum deputies and the like. However, the new legislation and its process of introduction has interrupted this steady, if small-scale shift. To begin with the senior managers have been getting conflicting 'messages' from the DES (DES 1989a, Sec. 4.3) and the NCC (NCC 1990, 1) respectively:

> The use of subjects to define the National Curriculum does not mean that teaching has to be organised and delivered within prescribed subject boundaries. Subject descriptions reflect the way in which the school curriculum is now most often planned and, in secondary schools, also organised. This reflects the advantages of such descriptions for clarity of presentation to those within and outside the education service, and as a means of ensuring that essential areas of the curriculum are properly covered.

> In due course, it is likely that schools will 'throw all the attainment targets in a heap on the floor and reassemble them in a way which provides for them the very basis of a whole curriculum'.

Where the DES appears reluctant to see subjects disappear the NCC positively promotes the idea. Thus the extent to which teachers feel licensed to promote cross-curricular links depends to some extent upon which 'official' text they read, and how they 'read' it. At an early staff INSET Day the Head of Science at Parkside, who is also a senior teacher referred to the cross-curricular elements of the National Curriculum. His department had spent a full day looking at the Science Statutory Orders in contrast with their existing curriculum for Key Stage 3.

Our experience has been that quite new elements have been

introduced and that's quite exciting. It may be these will be where you'll be able to get together with other departments.
(HOD, Science, Parkside, observation notes, 16 June 1989)

He clearly felt cross-curricular initiatives were going to provide new opportunities. However, *in practice*, the process whereby the National Curriculum is being introduced, 'a drip feed of Statutory Orders', each tightly timetabled for introduction immediately after their issue, has actually tended to reinforce the old, subject-based curriculum organization. As the Head of Mathematics at Flightpath put it,

I think the science department and maths department have both been sort of locked in a panic over their National Curriculum and we just haven't had the time or space to get together and look at the matches between them. We are still so busy sorting out our corner.
(HOD, Mathematics, Flightpath, interview, 6 June 1990)

The Head of Science at Flightpath, interviewed two days later, said something very similar when asked about the cross-curricular elements.

In this particular school, and I don't think it's atypical, inasmuch that departments tend to do their own thing, you simply don't have time to go and spend, meeting with other colleagues to discuss cross-curricular issues, in reality, the day-to-day life of a school is a pressurized one and you don't find the time to do that necessarily. Unless somehow the school takes it on board that this is an important aspect and we will allocate certain resources to do it.
(HOD, Science, Flightpath, interview, 8 June 1990)

And the Head of Science at Overbury school also pointed to the lack of time and 'other pressures' as common features of schools at present.

The head of geography and myself, sort of passing in the corridor, or over a cup of tea in the staffroom have made some mentions . . . myself and the head of home economics likewise and the head of CDT and maths. We are all aware that we do need to link up. But again it's down to the pressures which are exerted on us. It's the time factor.
(HOD, Science, Overbury, interview, 27 June 1990)

Gillborn (1991) finds a similar situation in his case study of New Bridge school. He says 'Teachers were caught in a paradoxical situation where the external demands on the school (from the DES, NCC and LEA) seemed to change rapidly, although there were precious few concrete facts', and, 'The most frequently adopted coping strategy involved a renewed emphasis on *teachers' indentities as subject specialists*' (p.15). The result is that cross-curricular matters will have to remain the responsibilty of senior management for whom, our data suggest, LMS has become the major concern. Where there is an interest in the 'dimensions', 'skills' and 'themes' that make up the cross-curricular elements of the National Curriculum (NCC 1990) the former two are 'delivered' by departments and it seems likely the themes may well be 'bolted on' as a carousel of non-subject specific offerings. In effect the 'implementation' process has interrupted what moves were in hand towards whole curriculum perspectives in schools.

All of this suggests that the substance of existing curriculum structures and the current institutional practices *may well not only remain in place but be reinforced by the way in which the National Curriculum is being introduced*. Thus in terms of the whole curriculum there seems little indication of any *need* for radical change, and it is difficult to support any argument that this is merely a period of transition. After all departmental structure and subject-based curricula have a long and powerful history that seems far more likely to feed off the National Curriculum structure rather than be weakened by it in any move into a whole curriculum.

Departments and their subject areas

The new process of curriculum development emerging out of the National Curriculum involves the replacement of local decisions based on direct experience, with general structures based on assumptions about 'normal' pacing and 'levels' of difficulty. What we want to suggest is that this stimulates a complex and sophisticated process of accommodation between the National Curriculum texts and existing assumptions and practices. The learning and changing that teachers and departments do in relation to the National Curriculum, like the learning that pupils do, involves making sense of the new in terms of past experiences and understandings. The ways in which the National Curriculum is construed are, in part, dependent upon existing subject paradigms and subject subcultures. The National Curriculum articulates with established theories-in-practice. Furthermore, this construction and interpretation is a social process, it is done with or in relation to colleagues. As a result the leadership of heads of department is important here. The skills and expertise of the heads of department, their capacity to make sense of change for or with colleagues, are a crucial resource, and a significant point of variation in the engagement of a department with National Curriculum texts.

The bell then went and the Mathematics INSET meeting broke up with nothing very definite resolved. On reflection it seemed to me the HOD had no worked out strategy and was continually getting involved in details and throwing in 'red herrings' without being aware how difficult it made it for people to follow any one line of argument. He was clearly flustered by the demands that were being made upon him, both as an HOD and in terms of the National Curriculum, and he regularly became confused about the principles behind the National Curriculum and the terms that are used. In many respects he would fit the image of 'one of the old school' in his attitude to students and the 'lower' members of his department. Retaining discipline of both seem to be an important part of his zeitgeist, avoiding losing face appears to operate as subtext to his relations with most parties.

(Mathematics Department, INSET day,
Parkside, observation notes, 19 June 1989)

Here the HOD found himself caught between the National Curriculum and his colleagues, he stood in part 'for' the National Curriculum, but reluctantly and unclearly. His uncertainty and perhaps frustration is evident in the following observation and quote:

There didn't appear to be any recognition that a notion of progression underlay the levels. This despite the fact that the Science HOD, (speaking at an INSET session to all the staff, some days earlier) had made a great play of this. The HOD Maths several times refuted observations about how science had begun to implement the NC by saying:

Ah yes, but maths is different. You can't do it that way because maths isn't like that.
(HOD, Mathematics, INSET day, Parkside, observation notes, 19 June 1989)

In effect this HOD failed to be an adequate interpreter of key texts for others and he clearly provoked a confusion between being *in* authority and being *an* authority. Like other innovations the National Curriculum can disrupt existing hierarchies, advantage some and disadvantage others. Information and understanding, 'authoritative readings', are at a premium in the process of accommodation. (Quite soon after this the head of mathematics resigned, explaining that, among other things, he felt unprepared to respond to the demands of the National Curriculum.)

The performance of the Head of Mathematics contrasted with that of the Head of Science in the same school discussing with the department 'levels' on a Science Department INSET Day.

I think we can characterize level 3 as understanding and level 4 as applying. Level 5, I have trouble interpreting that and fitting it into the progression. I think it's children devising their own experiment. Level 6 is collaborative and level 7 is the whole process.

You've really got to stretch your mind to see that progression.
(HOD, Science, Parkside, INSET day, observation notes, 8 June 1989)

Here was a strong interpretative approach with the HOD over-laying his own general view of progression through the levels of the National Curriculum. The effort was aimed at the accommodation of the levels into the existing conceptions of science in the department and the existing science syllabus. Interestingly this followed a session, organized by the LEA Science Adviser in which notions of progression were examined very closely, and strategies to help heads of department introduce the National Curriculum to their colleagues were also explored. However, the head of departments attempt to pre-structure and assist the process of curriculum development had to be set against other concerns and interest within the department.

For example, the head of department suggested that girls tended to be more interested in the biological sciences and therefore this was an important element in the first year to prevent them being put off. The problem was that this didn't fit with what was seen as the physics bias in AT1 (Attainment Target 1 in the Science Statutory Orders).

> We have to please Mr Baker, we can't be expected to please the kids as well.
>
> (Teacher, Science Department, Parkside, INSET day, observation notes, 8 June 1989)

What is being alluded to here is a mismatch of purposes, the academic/cognitive of the National Curriculum and the social/equal opportunities concerns of the members of the department. The irony of the humour reversed the direction of argument in 'official discourse' about the National Curriculum.

> What are we going to keep, throw out or add to what we've got.
>
> Should we keep the first-year course as it is but add a section called something like 'being a scientist?'
>
> Thing is we've really got to match the third year course to the fourth and fifth year syllabus.
>
> (HOD, Science, Parkside, INSET day, observation notes, 8 June 1989)

Mismatches of purpose are likely to give rise to a strategy of containment. In this case the basic conception of and structure of the department syllabus remain as the organizing principle to which the National Curriculum is 'added'.

> One of the things about this is that we can think up all sorts of logical progressions for these sections, but we've no way of knowing if the kids will see it like that.
>
> (HOD)

> If that's level 7 then we really ought to be teaching that in the third year.
>
> (Science teacher)

It seemed to me that the process was one of using the NC plus the existing course to develop a new course that had logics of progression that did not necessarily follow the NC logic, except in the case of AT1.

> We've never had the opportunity to sit down and get an overall view of what we are teaching, only occasionally look at sections together.

I don't want to lose the pollution topic. The kids really enjoy it and they should enjoy it, it's really important.

> (Science teacher, Parkside, INSET day,
> observation notes, 8 June 1989)

The process of interpretation and planning becomes all the more difficult when several different agendas are at work. In this example, the logics of progression in the National Curriculum are contrasted both with the departmental logic and the constructivist logic of the students and there is stubborn defence of the logic of enjoyment. The National Curriculum provides an irritant for review, but it must take its place within the bricolage of motives and theory that make up the pedagogic discourse within any department. In the case of some maths departments this may include a commitment to a particular, published scheme of work.

We're committed to SMP (the School Mathematics Project) 11–16 scheme, OK, the National Curriculum's come along but we're going to see where it's covered, we're going to use SMP. We're not going to, 'cos I know some schools have re-ordered it and put it into module blocks to fit in with the National Curriculum, but we've decided that time's been spent developing that scheme, the order of it is there for a reason. We're not going to mess up the scheme to make it fit into boxes in the National Curriculum, we're going to use the scheme, but make sure that we use additional material to cover the National Curriculum, and certainly when I left Shortcross, the same sort of thing was going on there. It was filling the holes that the scheme doesn't cover.

(HOD, Mathematics, Flightpath, interview, 3 November 1989)

This approach of retaining existing courses and 'filling in the holes' has been common to three of the mathematics departments we have looked at and anecdotal evidence suggests it is widespread where science and mathematics departments were already using widely available courses. But, if we dig further, what on the surface looks simply like a 'pick 'n' mix' approach actually contains rather deeper and more powerful strands.

The main mismatch is the statistics and probability section. SMP leaves that all 'til later on, you do a lot in the third, fourth and fifth year, and not very much in the first and second, and there's a lot of that in the National Curriculum lower down. So we've got to bring in resources, to cover that, which I think in a way is a good thing, because if you leave it too late, I mean it's the sort of skill which is used in so many other subjects and if it's not taught in maths, you've got to teach it in humanities, and so on and so forth.

(HOD, Mathematics, Flightpath, interview, 3 November 1989)

Here, views about appropriate progression and cross-curricular concerns actually cut across the National Curriculum document and raise difficulties for any form of straightforward 'implementation'. In the case of progression the model implicit in the National Curriculum would appear to be strongly preferred, but, a later comment indicates this may only be true of certain sections, in this case statistics and probability.

We've got to make sure we're covering it, we've got to report with reference to the National Curriculum. This is such a high profile thing that we've obviously got to be able to say what levels we're covering, when we're covering it, how we're covering it. But my commitment is to the scheme that we're using, and to make sure the National Curriculum is done within that but not to change the way we're working because of the National Curriculum.

(HOD, Mathematics, Flightpath, interview, 3 November 1989)

While there is the sense here of an external 'force' and there is a concern over reporting achievement there is also a strong commitment to an existing scheme of work and again accommodation is the outcome. In this case SMP is seen to have had a long and relatively successful history which has won the 'hearts and minds' of a significant number of maths teachers across the country. There is an unwillingness to take on the National Curriculum at those points where commitment to the scheme's view of progression remains high. A history of innovation and curriculum development in any school normally produces a set of professional 'side bets', these are not easily dislodged or surrendered in the face of changes generated externally – however forceful they may appear.

Thus departments have approached the National Curriculum in ways that also reflect the particularities of the subject area, its politics and its history. For example, the debate about integrated vs. separate subjects still remains pertinent, despite the existence of balanced science as a single subject in the National Curriculum.

> There are very definite subject boundaries and you can see it in the ATs. Some areas do lend themselves to cross-subject boundaries, like energy for example, but we've got to do our units in separate sciences.
>
>   (HOD, Science, Flightpath, interview, 15 June 1989)

The department has split Key Stage 3 into topics that tend to reflect the traditional three-science subject boundaries and, although the aim is to integrate the science elements, teachers' backgrounds make that difficult.

> We still talk in terms of biology, physics and chemistry, which is an antiquated traditional way, and I'm trying to get away from it. But you've got to live with facts and we've got staff here who are biologists, chemists and physicists, and whilst one tries to get towards balanced science, it's going to be a slow process I think.
>
>   (HOD, Science, Flightpath, interview, 11 July 1989)

Indeed, the histories and cultures of particular subjects may actually lead to different interpretations of possibility and constraint in the National Curriculum. At Parkside, for example, the science department view of progression was not shared by the mathematics department and they differed over when students were seen to be 'ready' for certain concepts and ideas. Interestingly, similar disjunctions are present in the Statutory Orders for the two subjects!

Observation notes from a mathematics department meeting at Parkside where the staff were trying to come to terms with the Statutory Orders indicates that there is a process of developing a collective reading of the Programmes of Study and the Attainment Targets; making sense by making meaning. In the process of pic 'n' mix, alluded to earlier, gaps in the text were identified, and the National Curriculum choices of what was crucial material was set against the collective wisdom and history of the department. The National Curriculum version of what is mathematics was not simply taken over. What the department members saw as 'basic' was retained, anything seen as 'redundant' removed.

They started going through the present syllabus trying to chop out what wasn't needed. There was a great deal of discussion about whether the National Curriculum required particular things to be taught or not.

I don't think I'd be happy throwing out something as basic as that.

(Teacher)

Well I suppose the first move is to find out what's redundant and then question whether it should be in or not.

(Teacher)

The snag is if we decide something is going to be redundant it can have a knock-on effect on the rest.

(HOD)

We say this is a minimum but there's a hell of a lot there.

(Teacher)

(Mathematics Department, Parkside, INSET day,
observation notes, 19 June 1989)

In this instance the teachers' priorities, experience and professional expertise were set over and against the structure, content and progression of school maths presented in the National Curriculum documents. The result is a lot of accommodation and minimal change. This may be what Duncan Graham (untill recently Chair of the NCC) meant by teachers making the National Curriculum their own. But the interesting, difficult and, for some teachers, frustrating thing, is to know where the limits of this process of accommodation will be set.

Now we've reached the situation where we've done year one and we've got the topics written, planned out in every detail, which can run again next year no problem. We've even got assessment worked out in relation to it a little bit. But not too much 'cos no one's given us any guidance on that. But the second year, the first topic is biological and I've got no one to write it. The second topic is a completely new collection of things that we need to put in there because they are in the National Curriculum. But they're things that we'd actually eliminated from the first and second year work, over the years, because we decided they were a bit too difficult, and were better handled later on.

> (HOD, Science, Parkside, interview, 6 June 1990)

It seems from data so far that the question of progression produces the most obvious writerly responses (see pp.10–12) from mathematics and science teachers. There is certainly no passive acceptance of, or mere adaptation to, the progression identified in the National Curriculum texts. It is common to find that collective interpretations and strategies emerge in the 'spaces' left by these texts, and these may be developed through social and professional networks in LEAs, subject associations, etc. Thus in some departments incoherence in the text may become latitude and latitude becomes incorporation and eventually accommodation. Some teachers may be oppressed by the National Curriculum text but we find considerable evidence of creative responses.

> Well . . . I mean there are two philosophies towards the National Curriculum. One is to see it as totally prescriptive and to go through the levels and work out activities to fit the levels, and the other is to see how far the National Curriculum comes into the work that you're already doing, and I think that . . . I think there's a tremendous lack of direction, and lack of clarity in this respect, which is in some ways I suppose part of the sort of politicial negotiation about the exact position of the National Curriculum, and a tendency to panic . . . but we've got through that . . . largely because a friend of mine is an advisory teacher in the Borough of Lewisham and has a lot of access to ILEA . . . in-service and so on . . . and through talking with her . . . we've come to the conclusion that we're going to . . . we think that our basic approach is correct . . . and that we're going to look at our approach and see where the National Curriculum and the profile components fit in to our activities and . . . rather to concentrate on developing a good lower school curriculum, and so that's what we've decided to do. We've decided to formulate schemes of work in which . . . we have the sort of scheme of work in the centre . . . then radiating out from it, with arrows, the areas of the National Curriculum that will be covered. (HOD, English, Pankhurst, interview, 28 November 1989)

Departments in context

Staffing the national curriculum

One of the many problems involved in relating exhortations of change to the world of schooling is the tendency for policy texts to be written in terms of an assumption that ideal conditions for change apply across the schooling system. Texts fail to account for the fact that in most schools change will take place against a backdrop of unforeseen, unforeseeable and unavoidable difficulties; put succinctly, schools are very diverse. The question of staffing is just one of several vicissitudes that are routinely ignored. In these texts the implicit model of the department in change is that of a group of experienced, fulltime, stable, specialists. Typically for schools in London, and especially for departments of science and mathematics, such an assumption is untenable. The following quotes from our case study schools make the point well:

> We now have an art teacher teaching science and a CDT teacher, we've got an information technology teacher teaching science, and we've got a mathematician teaching science . . . what we can look at is pulling Larry Jones, who's gallantly struggled with physics through the fifth year, with no physics particularly in his background, to fill in things a bit. Up from 12 periods to 25.
>
> (HOD, Science, Flightpath, interview, 6 June 1990)

> So we're going to have to draw in people from science, English . . . Mrs Saltzman, the Head Teacher, who is an English teacher, wanted to come in and teach some maths with the first years, and we've got, I think there may be somebody from PE, so we've got a variety of people, one of whom is totally non-mathematically based.
>
> *Interviewer*: Does that mean that the balance of non-specialists as against specialists is shifting towards non-specialists at the moment?
>
> Yes, I would say it is, 'cos I think that the department has had three and a half specialists . . . and we're moving along to about three specialists and four non-specialists.
>
> (HOD, Mathematics, Overbury, interview, 19 June 1990)

I've lost all three people who were able to teach biology up to
fifth year level ... I've lost the two best teachers of lower school
science. I've lost the two people who've put the most into the
preparation of the National Curriculum, schemes of work,
assessment and so on, in the last twelve months.

(HOD, Science, Parkside, interview, 6 June 1990)

The presence of non-specialist teachers, the use of supply
teachers or part-timers, high rates of staff turnover, illness and
absence, all affect the capacity of a department to respond and to
plan for the National Curriculum and will influence the form and
nature of the response and the degree of planning. For example,
the presence of a number of non-specialists in the science and
mathematics departments we studied meant that one HOD felt it
necessary to produce fairly closed, pre-prepared curriculum
materials. There is clearly a delicate and indeterminate balance
that is sought between communality and individuality, prescription and autonomy in the production of units of work.

That will sort of give a whole package then, provide a whole
package for the teacher. I think that will be a useful situation if
they've got something they can pick up and use. Now the one
thing, the one danger is that you're being very prescriptive and
you're telling people what to teach, but then the National Curriculum is doing that anyway. It's just all we're trying to do, all
I'm trying to do is to achieve some kind of conformity over
what is taught, which is again a requirement of the National
Curriculum, in a way which allows the teacher to actually
maximize his or her efficiency, I think, in terms of time, usage
of time, and delivering the goods. I don't think staff, I'm sure
staff are not worried about being constrained by this approach
that we're taking. I feel that they think that it would be supportive if we did have this kind of approach. Once we've written
these units, it's not something that is written in tablets of stone,
it's something that will change, and as I said earlier on, we're
going to review this lot in a year's time. (HOD, Science,
Flightpath, interview, 11 July 1989)

Indeed the Education Reform Act, 1988, has actually increased
the pressure that teachers feel under as a result of shortages.
Concern over external checks, whether via inspections, SATs or
parental and governor scrutiny has changed the way in which

schools have tried to cope with and disguise teacher shortages, lack of good supply and so on. Now departments are accountable for appropriate delivery of the National Curriculum they must take responsibility for contingent problems not of their making and often not within their control.

> In the past you could get away with staff shortages by reallocation of staff to exam classes and the first and second years. I'm afraid they were suffering, but it wasn't an obvious sufferance in terms of we didn't have to tell anybody, you know, it happened, it went on cracks were papered over. OK, the kids didn't get such a good deal in the first year but by the fourth year hopefully things would have been sorted out, if you didn't go for too long, kind of thing. And that is the same situation now, but now we've got to as I say we're open to observation as to what we're doing because these kids are not getting the full National Curriculum treatment, and we're caught both ways.
>
> (HOD, Science, Flightpath, interview, 8 June 1990)

Such problems of continuity and expertise in subject areas are compounded in many departments by the fact that many teachers, especially senior staff, have multiple involvements in aspects of the implementation of the ERA. This is rather starkly evidenced by the position of the Head of Science at Parkside:

> I am senior teacher, I am supposed to be a member of the management team, but I can't go to the management meetings because they're on Tuesday afternoons. And I can't do that because there isn't a physics teacher to take the sixth form then and I have to take them then. So I'm missing out on the management meetings. I'm being given things that I'm supposed to look at, which is the kind of overall implementation of National Curriculum across the school. Just keeping a kind of timetable of implementation and things, and keeping myself informed of what different departments are doing, so I can still input that at management meetings. But I can't start to do that because I'm working, I mean I'm reckoning on about a 70 hour week over this term so far. I'm sort of coming out at 10.30, four evenings a week, which I'm not too keen on.
>
> (HOD, Science, Parkside, interview, 18 October 1989)

Many teachers find the National Curriculum an additional burden in their already stressful working lives. In all the case study schools the implementation of the National Curriculum took its toll in terms of morale, commitment and energy.

> Well most of them were worn out ... we had a meeting last night, and I noticed two people were nearly asleep and I don't think it was because I was particularly boring or, you know, 'cos everybody was taking part. But, you see, very often the meetings are at the end of the day and I have one member of department who is a senior teacher, who is head of fifth and first year, so you can imagine what sort of state she's in most of the time. She's absolutely exhausted, and my probationer, who is now on, you know, five free periods plus a form group, and ... she's just come out of her probation actually, 'cos she did it from Christmas to Christmas, or she will have done by the end of this term, and she's carrying on very gamely, but obviously she gets extremely tired. I mean I think it's fair to say that teachers are very very tired, and very, quite tense.
>
> (HOD, English, Pankhurst, interview, 28 November 1989)

Furthermore, the particular constitution and characteristics of a staff is an important factor in coping with change. Different schools are more or less well provided with an infrastructure of both experience and commitment. This applies equally to the teaching and the ancillary staff.

> We have quite a lot of part-timers. I don't know whether Miss Chateau told you, we've got, I think it's 10 part-timers, they're very good and they do... you know, when they're here they work jolly hard, but it does put extra pressure on people who're fulltime, because it means a lot of the responsibilities have to be shared between fewer people.
>
> (Deputy Head, Pankhurst, interview, 15 June 1990)

> Science as an active base subject would just stop without those lab techs. They're vital to what we're trying to achieve in the classroom.
>
> (HOD, Science, Flightpath, interview, 30 October 1989)

> So I've been six months without him, and a second colleague, went downhill in April, who is still off. And I really don't know

when he is going to return. So I could be starting off next year,
not only with lab alterations, but also possibly a fulltime
member of staff down as well. So since January I've had a
succession of supply teachers, which have covered altogether
quite a number of classes, including three first-year classes.
Now these kids are following or supposedly following the
National Curriculum.

(HOD, Science, Overbury, interview, 27 June 1990)

It would probably be a generous overstatement to say that the
introduction of the National Curriculum is informed by a theory
of innovation, clearly it is not. In fact our research indicates that
it is governed as much by serendipity, ad hockery and chaos as by
planning. But if a theory were to be attributed to the perception
of change presented by teachers it would come closest to a power-
coercive strategy. Perhaps more accurately it is change by a
process of attrition. Teachers feel under pressure and are experi-
encing considerable overload and stress. Senior staff are weighed
down by multiple roles and the impact of multiple and diverse
innovations. Even so, subject or pedagogical allegiances, and
what might be called 'professional responsibility' strongly medi-
ate the policy texts of the National Curriculum (see 'Being a
professional', below)

The long, dark shadow of assessment

Do we stick to the lines down here or are we more ambitious. I
mean, as time goes on we shall change and this will probably
change anyway (referring to the National Curriculum document). And we can't tell what this means because of SATs.
[Standard Attainment Tasks].

(HOD, Mathematics, Parkside, observation notes,
INSET Day, 16 June 1989)

The question of reporting pupil achievement and the linked and
equally uncertain question of what form assessment will take,
tends to make them the 'jokers in the pack'. Although many of the
teachers we interviewed spoke relatively positively about the
concept of a National Curriculum and sometimes welcomed their
own subject's Statutory Orders, the response to the prospects of
national testing was unanimously negative. Fear, loathing and

dread were the normal reactions. The fear of the unknown fed by the 'horror story' press coverage about the piloting of the SATs made planning and change all the more difficult.

This is a personal view, but I think the NC document is quite exciting. There are a lot of things in there that should have been in there before, like the emphasis on multi-cultural texts, I think it's good. To actually put it in means that people are going to look at it and do it, and I think the knowledge about language, a lot of it, although we have done some of it already, the talk about dialect and the historical development of language and so on, I think is very interesting and should be there. But as regards testing, I think it's going to have absolutely devastating effects on schools for precisely the reasons that we were talking about.

(HOD, English, Pankhurst, interview, 28 November 1989)

At the moment I'm almost ignoring the national testing, because we know so little about it. You can't work towards something you don't know anything about. I think provided the levels have been covered by the time they get to the testing stage, it doesn't matter whether they're covered in the order that they're put down in the National Curriculum or not. I mean obviously once the testing starts it will have implications. I mean we'll know what's being required in the tests and obviously that is going to affect to some extent the teaching, but I don't see the tests as the be-all and end-all of the National Curriculum. I mean you're educating people, not just teaching them to pass tests.

(HOD, Mathematics, Flightpath, interview,
3 November 1989)

Problems. Well I think it's just the amount of it and a major problem is the recording and assessment which again, it's a lack of clarity because you don't know whether to go ahead and develop methods of assessment and recording when possibly they may be disregarded in the end. You don't know in how much detail to go into those, and in this LEA, if you've spoken in other schools, you'll know there's a primary language record that's been developed and a working group that are looking at that.

(HOD, English, Pankhurst, interview, 28 November 1989)

I think there are still enormous problems with record keeping and assessment . . . It's just a vast problem. I don't know what the solution is. I mean, the National Curriculum is so detailed. Do you assess everything, do you spend your whole time assessing? Where do you teach if you assess everything?

(HOD, Mathematics, Flightpath, interview, 6 June 1990)

How far 'teaching to the test' can be avoided will depend a great deal upon the outcome of the work being done on assessment by the various SATs development groups. Many teachers have expressed considerable concern about any system of assessment that leans strongly towards the testing rather than assessment paradigm (Troman 1989). Within teaching in the UK over the past 20 years, there has been a steady move away from a testing paradigm with new forms of assessment, including formative and diagnostic, gaining wide acceptance (Bowe and Whitty 1989). Not suprisingly then, at this stage, many teachers are choosing to ignore the possibility that the testing paradigm will be preferred and they are developing approaches to the curriculum that would make 'implementation' of such a system very difficult.

Interviewer: In terms of the actual attainment targets themselves, I take it that you're not particularly following through in the order that they're in . . .

No, this is something that we changed really, I think, because first of all you think, National Curriculum, you've got to follow it through in the order that it is, but then people went on courses, you came in and we started to discuss it and we thought, well this is a bit silly really, they're not going to be formally tested until the end of the third key stage, that's right, isn't it? So we thought well it's much more sensible to follow the order, as we think, as SMP think or as we think, and then to just check up whether the attainment targets have been covered. As long as we know where they are in the booklets, we should be able to record it.

(HOD, Mathematics, Flightpath, interview, 5 July 1989)

Concern over assessment introduces an interesting ambivalence in relation to the National Curriculum text. On the one hand there is a strongly stated strategy of containment outlined, SMP and teacher experience interrupting the Statutory Orders views of progression and possibly content. Then there looms the spectre of of assessment and the HOD sees the possibility that this may confound the assertion of the departmental view of appropriate progression. This may well be the place to look for the limits of accommodation. The idea that teachers can make the curriculum their own does not take adequate account of the constraints that may arise from a national testing regime. Indeed there are already indications that such testing is being anticipated and is influencing classroom teaching, which the Government may well intend it to do.

> One thing that is materializing is that we're tending, in the light of experience with the National Curriculum, we're actually tending to try and gear lessons more so now to attainment targets than perhaps we were before.
>
> (HOD, Science, Flightpath, interview, 8 June 1990)

> And I mean there's also the danger that you let the assessment take over your lesson content, take over the lesson in fact. I mean, if you're assessing oral work, and oral skills, you can't actually join very readily, in oral groups, if you're assessing at the same time, because one requires you to stand back a bit and be, you know, totally objective. And the other sort of, if you, perhaps if a group's stuck or whatever, requires you to launch in and take part. And just to do it for GCSE is quite something. To think of doing it over the school, I think it creates a tremendous amount of tension and anxiety and, but there's also the tension and anxiety about wanting to do the right thing, because we all feel that this, this one mark, and this is it, this is your child at level something, is totally and utterly wrong, educationally, in terms of the development of the child, not giving an accurate picture in many cases. So we all want to put in the diagnostics, to give the complete picture of the child, but at the same time are tremendously aware of the pressures upon us.
>
> (HOD, English, Pankhurst, interview, 28 November 1989)

The more recent interviews indicate that the particular situation of departments at the time of the issuing of the Statutory Orders can affect their response to the National Curriculum. Thus the science departments at Flightpath and Parkside, took the opportunity to rework their first two years' curriculum. In both cases they combined aspects of their existing courses with the National

Curriculum to produce new, unit-based courses. However, at Parkside the course created has retained its integrity while at Flightpath the National Curriculum is beginning to make inroads into the original intentions.

> *Interviewer*: Do you feel in the process of getting closer and closer to the attainment targets, in some respects, and is that a process of getting closer and closer to teaching it as it is in the national curriclum. Because originally you tried to get some sort of compromise between some of the work you were already doing and the National Curriculum. You tried to use the opportunity if you like, to rewrite the first two years, in a way that took the best of what you already had and the best bits of the National Curriculum and meshed them in together. Are you finding that inevitably you're being, as you look at the attainment targets, and as you go back and refer to the folders, the National Curriculum folders, that you've been pulled closer and closer towards the National Curriculum.
>
> Yes, I think that's a fair statement. . .
>   (HOD, Science, Flightpath, interview, 8 June 1990)

Both the science department at Flightpath and that at Parkside have suffered from considerable pressure on staff throughout the year but even so Parkside was able to develop a clear, independent logic to its course and also drew in the third year to their planning. This has given them the confidence and foundation to write units that retain their own original aspirations for science in the school. In contrast Flightpath has been keen to ensure a tight system of assessment, for the most part using GASP (Graded Assessment in Science Project). This has resulted in the putting together of regular tests that draw people back to the levels of attainment as a 'source book'. Their concentration upon assessment has had the unintended consequence of making them more dependent upon the National Curriculum text than they set out to be.

Being a 'professional'

The subject specific and assessment concerns which were articulated by the teachers in the case-study schools, tended to be reinforced by more general and deeper-seated worries about the long term erosion of teachers' professionalism. While some may, resignedly, accept their position has been publicly undermined, attempts by the Government and DES to invade all areas of the curriculum, assessment and pedagogy may well produce far less of a feeling of resignation. In time it seems likely that the 'talking up' of the teaching profession by Kenneth Baker (Minister of Education 1986–9) and his immediate successor, John McGregor, may well be placed alongside the comments of the then Prime Minister, Margaret Thatcher, as grounds for claiming a greater professional role for teachers in the new ERA. At the moment, however, there is evidence within our case-study schools, that the question of 'doing a professional job' can be set over and against the lack of teaching experience among the Government's curriculum planners. The whole notion of teacher professionalism therefore remains to provide a powerful critical vocabulary of aspects of the National Curriculum.

One manifestation of this is a degree of scepticism which seems to be common among the teachers in the case-study schools who are 'receiving' the National Curriculum, especially in the light of the delays in disseminating materials. This has created extra 'space' for the media to 'interfere' with the message. But there is a good deal more to this than delays and the interference of the media. Central is the continued feeling of an implicit attack on their professionalism that the initial development and subsequent 'implementation' of the National Curriculum are seen to constitute. The translation of the legislation into the language of education is being conducted on one level by the National Curriculum Council and on another through the Subject Working Parties. Teachers varyingly aim their scepticism at these two bodies, while retaining a deep sense of both scepticism and resentment of the Government's role. To some extent this has meant teachers have allowed 'them' a licensed autonomy, to stand Dale's notion (Dale 1989) on its head, to operate in the educational world. This has been dependent on 'them' showing a degree of credibility in the teachers' eyes. Scepticism in this instance privileges the text and allows teachers to express a certain degree of tolerance, to view it as being capable of a benevolent interpretation. However, such tolerance can prove to be fragile, especially where the legislation and/or the 'translation' in NCC or DES documents fails to show an appreciation of the school setting. Maintaining 'street credibility' with the teaching profession is unlikely to be an easy path. There are strong residues of collective resentment that require very little to trigger off small pockets of resistance. The mismatches between the National Curriculum structures and school resources (time, teachers, materials, space) are a particular source of worry and antipathy. On the one hand many teachers feel that the National Curriculum is asking them to do many things that they are already doing, while assuming that they were not. On the other they consider it is asking them to do things that simply cannot be done within the constraints within which they must operate. In both these respects they feel affronted. For some teachers the requirements of the National Curriculum, taken as a whole, seem irreconcilable and unachievable. The Deputy Head of Pankhurst expressed some of these feelings:

Interviewer: So how do you feel about the National Curriculum, in relation to all that. Making you look at what you're doing, change what you're doing?

Well again, I resent the fact that the public image is that we weren't doing most of these things anyway, because in this school we'd always made everybody do, I mean it seems so obvious, everybody did English and maths. But the media image is that they didn't. Virtually all the girls had always done modern language, they'd all had to do a science, we'd already moved to the integrated science course, because we wanted to counteract the fact that we thought there were still too many of them doing biology. We'd already introduced technology, and we were trying very very hard to positively discriminate so that girls would go into it, we were already doing all these things. So I mean I don't necessarily resent the National Curriculum, I just am cross that people think we weren't doing a lot of it in the first place.

Interviewer: Do all those things going on mean that you're having to make less accommodation in terms of dealing with the National Curriculum?

I would have thought we're having to do less than some schools, yes. But having said that I mean the squeeze on the timetable is, I'm worried about how it's going to go.

Interviewer: What sort of things?

Well I mean as the working parties come out, I mean, right, science. They expect every girl to do double science eventually, so it's 20 per cent they reckon. Even if they only do single – the exceptions might be allowed to only do single – they want 12 per cent. English want to hang on to the amount they have, which is over actually the amount that perhaps the National Curriculum would have suggested. History and geography have come out, haven't they, demanding more timetable time than they traditionally get in the lower school. Now if you start adding all these things up it's not manageable, if you're still teaching them all these discrete subjects . . . I'm slightly worried, although I know the Head thinks perhaps I'm worrying unnecessarily, but at the moment the second foreign language is only available to about half the year, and done on linguistic ability and I'm not sure how far that's a viable position with, with the idea of entitlement curriculum and common curriculum. I'm not sure about that. So I think the Government's being Machiavellian, I think they want to increase the working day because I can't see us getting it all done, unless there's a sort of major rethink of sort of cross-curricular issues and that would be so major, and involve so much reorientating of people's thoughts and I can't see it happening.

(Deputy Head, Pankhurst, interview, 15 June 1990)

But the pressures upon doing a good, professional job, also arise from the change process itself.

Lack of time, it was all done in too much of a rush.

(HOD, Mathematics, Flightpath, interview, 6 June 1990)

Insufficient time was given prior to the introduction of the National Curriculum. There just hasn't been time to do it all.

(HOD, Science, Overbury, interview, 27 June 1990)

The pace of change required by the government timetable clearly fails to recognize the complexity of the teachers' task or the demands involved in making a thorough and coherent response to the National Curriculum. Teachers feel a whole variety of reponsibilities to their students. The National Curriculum may actually cut across some of these. The multi-faceted nature of change is not fully appreciated and the teacher's sense of professional responsibility does not begin and end with the National

Curriculum, or with teaching and learning. The role of the teacher is broad and diffuse and often ambiguous. The National Curriculum is in some circumstances a diversion from other things of more immediate importance. There are other innovations to be coped with and groups of children to be taught *here and now*. What may seem slowness to react or failure to plan is often the result of carefully thought out professional decisions to do other things. The National Curriculum can actually be seen to 'get in the way'.

The Baker days [occasional, whole school in-service days, named after the then Minister of Education], disjoint everything. I mean today I saw my fourth year class, I'll see them again in almost three weeks' time, 'cos all we've got is half-term, but we've got a Baker day on Friday, we've got two Baker days after the half-term, and that shifts the whole pattern of lessons, I don't see those kids for three weeks. I mean we've just got them going, I've just done what, seven weeks of this term, just got the momentum built up, and I won't see them for three weeks. It takes so much effort to build up the momentum of the kids handing things in and work coming back, and you just get everything rolling, actually sort of producing things, a few detentions and they realise you're serious and, okay, you can keep it going, once you start it but if you break for three weeks . . .

(HOD, Science, Parkside, interview, 18 October 1989)

Having said all that, we've also got profiling, and I mean I know the Government have now said we don't have to do profiling, but we'd already started profiling, or we'd already planned to start profiling. Therefore profiling is going ahead. And it literally needs minutes, tens of minutes, we need to channel, to explain how to evaluate what they're doing, which essentially is what they've got to do, if they're going to do a self-evaluation, fill in a check list of – 'I've done this, I've shown I can do this skill', which is part of what it is, 'cos it is about them appreciating the development of their own . . . Then it needs a huge chunk of time out of the lesson time. We can't give them that because you're having a struggle to complete the course and we're supposed to be doing that with the first years, with the fourth years and obviously we've got to put something together for the fifth years. We're not addressing that one, we've fudged that we've sort of, we talked round it at the last department meeting sort of literally postponed discussion . . .

(HOD, Science, Parkside, interview, 18 October 1989)

An even bigger problem is the third-year course and that will need an even bigger revision of the units of work, and the preparation of units of work. It needs detailed planning next summer term, and outline planning from September. The SATs are coming early in the summer term. This is reassembling the motorbike, and this is where we find out whether we've got a whole load of bits left over, and the whole damn thing will fall to pieces as soon as we try to operate it.

(HOD, Science, Parkside, interview, 6 September 1990)

Professional judgements over the required pace of change, its complexity and strong feelings of responsibility to the students are seen to be placed in conflict by the various demands that have been imposed from outside.

And already staff are saying, we're rushing through this, we're trying to get it done, and I'm conscious of the fact that whilst we've written month-long modules, units, we're not as far into that as we ought to be at this stage. It seems to me, we're behind, because of various things, it's a new course, staff haven't done some of the experiments before, they're much more lethargic in their approach because of that, I mean they are trying obviously, they're doing their best, but they are teaching new material and it takes time to actually get that moving efficiently through the department. And I feel that we're already behind schedule.

(HOD, Science, Flightpath, interview, 30 October 1989)

We are slow, and I could have predicted at the beginning of the year that we would have been slow because of what we're trying to do, but we're slower than that even. And then we have the problem what do we do for year eight? Presumably we carry on with the first-year course, into year eight, and by the time they get into year nine, we're perhaps going to be half a term adrift, or even longer, even further adrift, and then we've got the SATs which will occupy who knows four, six weeks of lessons, in the spring term or something, or the summer, early summer term. How on earth do we deliver this programme that we've got outlined which doesn't allow for any slowness on our part?

(HOD, Science, Flightpath, interview, 8 June 1990)

Thus several of our respondents expressed very strongly their sense of professional doubt, their lack of belief and trust in the change process set by the Government for the National Curriculum. Many people interviewed suggested that the Government were actually asking them to do a less than professional job with the National Curriculum. This rapid pace of change, the lack of support and facilities, inadequate staffing, the experience of innovation overload (Apple 1983) and contradictions between innovations of different kinds means people feel that in order to get by they have to botch and make do, skimp and compromise. For many this meant they felt pupils were getting a raw deal. The National Curriculum was getting in the way of good teaching, diverting attention, time and energy from the task at hand – teaching – or simply making impossible demands.

Managing the National Curriculum

In the heat and dust of technical talk about change in schools it is usual to find talk about curriculum matters conducted separately from talk about other changes, like LMS. There are different arenas of debate and increasingly sharp divisions of labour and expertise in schools. But, although the priorities created by LMS are significantly different from those invested in the National Curriculum innovation, LMS may well affect what is possible in terms of the curriculum and pedagogy. For example, the following exchange took place in a Curriculum Council meeting at Flightpath Comprehensive.

I'm sure all this is the same for a lot of other schools and shouldn't we just decide upon the needs and be prepared to overspend.

(Head of third year)

But that's the unreal world and it's not negotiable and you might as well accept that. I can assure you that there'll be no expansion in Westway [LEA] and I could take you through the detailed economics of the formula and the rest. We've got high idealism and we'd need higher resources than we've got. It's as straightforward as that.

(Head)

The Head then gave an example:

If it means you have to change your methods then that's what you'll have to do. I mean chalk and talk is cheaper than a sort of individualized carousel and we'll just have to make those choices.

(Flightpath, Curriculum Council meeting, observation notes, 5 March 1990)

But, 'chalk and talk' may orient learning far more towards the content of the curriculum and away from the development of skills and critical capacities in students. Key in this respect is the size of teaching groups.

The question of group size is being forced upon us by formula funding. There's a sort of remorseless logic about this.

(Senior Deputy, Flightpath, Curriculum Council meeting, observation notes, 5 March 1990)

In times of financial austerity when school budgets often contain little room for flexibility, difficult choices are having to be made. The heads of department at Flightpath were soon to be confronted with the implications of the 'remorseless logic' of group size:

A last-minute meeting was called, after school, an emergency meeting of heads of department. The implications if you didn't increase group size, on all the other areas of the curriculum, were so enormous, that the four or five of us who were actually affected, who had gone along with a defensive attitude about our particular subject, everybody said in the end, well given what we've heard, we haven't really got a case to argue. So larger groups aren't ideal, but the other things are needed more.

(HOD, Mathematics, Flightpath, interview, 6 June 1990)

Consequently, decisions about the best and most appropriate form of delivery for the National Curriculum were subordinated to budget setting and vocabularies of institutional survival. Again there are diverse and contradictory responsibilities interwoven here. Budgetary responsibilities are set over and against educational ones. And 'the immediate', doing the best for students in classrooms *now*, is set over and against longer term questions of survival. For the subject teacher and heads of department timescales are typically short and hectic, it is often a case of preparing for the immediate task in hand rather than spending the time reflecting upon the options and coming to terms with the National Curriculum:

> It's not often that you have the opportunity to sit back and survey what you've done, and think about the future because you're so wrapped up in preparing tomorrow's lesson or preparing for a meeting or doing something that is imminent almost. That seems to be the ball game that we're into.
> (HOD, Science, Flightpath, interview, 11 July 1989)

While the financial planners in the senior management team may be in a position to take a longer view their critique of staff 'short-termism' may well breed further resentment and place curriculum concern directly in conflict with budgetary concerns.

Part of the new logic, set up by LMS, brings a growing recognition that staffing and curriculum planning are themselves market related; in particular, financial planning is now beginning to reflect the exigencies of the teacher labour market. We have already talked about some of the problems created for the National Curriculum implementation by the constraints arising from staffing, but shortages of specialist staff also means that money has to be spent to attract applicants for 'problem' vacancies. These expenditures have to be met from the schools' devolved budgets and, of course, reduce the funds available for other purposes.

> In the department we have an incentive A, which according to the shadow structure for salaries and scales, we shouldn't have, but we are in that position, we had to do it, to get the right people and the Head was quite happy to do that, spend the extra money to get the right people.
> (HOD, Science, Flightpath, interview, 8 June 1990)

To become perhaps a head of science as the next thing to do after being in charge of biology. It's not as easy for a biologist as it is perhaps for a phsyical scientist, because of the climate of the lack of physical scientists. I mean people in schools who have money to spend in perhaps in a constrained way under LMS, do not wish to put scale D resources, into a biologist possibly, they'd rather use that D to attract a physical scientist.

(HOD, Science, Flightpath, interview, 8 June 1990)

But all these came really together, we had these consecutive maternity leaves and then we had a death and we had a variety of supply teachers, which understandably were not the best but we couldn't get anybody else, because they just couldn't afford to live in the area, or they weren't mathematics teachers. So it had an affect.

(HOD, Mathematics, Overbury, interview, 9 October 1989)

In science in particular teacher shortages mean having to meet the market price. But this picture is also extending to other subject areas and schools are faced with the dilemma of deciding which replacements are the most important. It may therefore be that the labour market for teachers, in conjunction with National Curriculum, produces an even more rigid subject hierarchy. Core first, then foundation, and lastly . . .?

We're stuck, we're advertising, but I mean obviously we've passed resignation dates, so the chance of appointing someone, and it's on an A, what's that worth? I wrote the job specification out last night. I wouldn't take the job for £500 or £800 over the main professional grade, it's a joke. The Head's made a modern languages appointment, which he's had to make on a B in order to get someone, so he's done the same thing again. He's under tremendous pressure. He's got to have staff.

(HOD, Science, Parkside, interview, 6 June 1990)

This is especially pertinent in our case study schools where the 'London factor' is having an increasing impact. Experienced teachers are leaving and new teachers are difficult to attract.

It's this movement away from London, it seems there's almost a sort of inevitability of people reaching their mid-thirties, or forty and moving out, moving back to where they came from.

(HOD, Science, Parkside, interview, 6 June 1990)

And the use of incentive payments to attract new staff has a knock on effect on the morale and commitment of existing staff.

If you're someone who's been slogging your guts out for ten years and you're on an A and you see someone pulled in who's no better than you, simply because the school can't get any-body, you feel a sense of grievance maybe. It's market forces at their most brutal.

(HOD, Science, Parkside, interview, 6 June 1990)

But the introduction of LMS is not simply a matter of devolving budgets, it also involves changes in school governance and is related to new relations between schools and their clients. In terms of the former, the department is now much more closely coupled and potentially more directly accountable to governing bodies. Governors have powers of overseeing of the school cur-riculum and the curriculum is also now a crucial part of a school's marketability. Parents, as clients, have to be considered. In some ways schools have to be more parent orientated than child orientated.

For example, while this might be the ideal curriculum situation from their point of view, the realities are that we do have to provide an image to fulfil the requirement of the governors and the parents and I think one of the hardest areas that staff are trying to come to grips with at the moment is the reality that the governors and especially the parents, have a far greater say and influence in what goes on in the school, than they've ever experienced in the past. Fortunately we have an excellent relationship with our governors, and they listen very carefully to the advice given to them through the senior managers, and we in turn try to take on board the heads of departments' wishes and concerns over the National Curricu-lum. So it's all about educating staff as well.

(Senior teacher, Flightpath, interview, 23 March 1990)

Clearly teachers have always been aware of and variously attuned to the particular needs of their pupils, but in a period where market forces and competition between schools may pro-duce a greater fluidity in enrolment and recruitment, curriculum and pedagogy may have to be monitored and rethought more frequently.

Our present fourth year, when you look at the ability of that year and our present first years, there's a remarkable difference, because we've become more popular, we're able to draw in more able children, so we've had to try and develop a fairly flexible approach to all of this. Hence my comment that the present first year, the National Curriculum year, may well change to the books earlier. We may even say well, half of the year change to the books, the other half carry on with the booklets, it may be that. It depends on the circumstances and what we agree as a department.

(HOD, Mathematics, Overbury, interview, 19 June 1990)

However, while the rhetoric of LMS celebrates the autonomy and control that is given to schools by the devolution of budgets, this rhetoric often serves to obscure the overall financial limits that are imposed upon school funding. The National Curriculum is being implemented in a period when spending on schools, in real terms, is declining and LEAs do not have a free hand in the setting of their education budgets. (These limits have been further reduced by the £35 million cut from education budgets in the poll-capped local authorities. Neither of the authorities in the research sample have been capped.) There is no obvious direct relationship between levels of funding and changes that schools are required to make. Indeed for schools in poll-capped authorities or schools losing numbers in the competitive education market place the National Curriculum may be a luxury that they can ill-afford. Financial management is often a euphemism for cuts and saving.

Now next term, if Malcolm gets the B, which I can't believe that he will not get, then he's on the A, so he'll get the B, what's happened to the A. That will go into the LMS, so they're saving money because they're having to save money. I'm sure a few years ago it would have been, there's an A there, we'll use it up, make sure somebody gets that.

(HOD, Mathematics, Overbury, interview, 19 June 1990)

In this instance flexibility in the overall budget may work against the retention of staff who see careers and promotions being closed down. The long-term consequences may be a steady skewing of staffing budgets in favour of the core and foundation subjects, with the added complication of what is being 'tested' by the SATs helping to decide upon the final budget structure. In all of this student needs, the commitment to a Whole Curriculum and responding to the consumers would have to take a back seat. The National Curriculum would be working in direct contradiction to other aspects of the ERA. The 'choices' for schools are thus set in such a way that 'rational decision making' must operate in an irrational world.

CONCLUSION

In this chapter we have stressed and highlighted some commonly expressed problems of and responses to the National Curriculum. In doing so we have also tried to show that the pattern of problems and response vary between schools and departments. On the one hand such variation reflects a shifting political debate within the bodies of the State (the DES, the NCC, the ministers of education and even the Prime Minister) about prescriptiveness, the subject-based curriculum, national testing and the extent of the 'educational' market. On the other hand, in the context of the schools, it reflects the different *capacities, contingencies, commitments and histories* of these institutions. In concluding we want to consider the developing histories of the National Curriculum and the institutional settings and their relationship and discuss briefly the analytical validity of the four concepts for understanding the processes of change.

Capacities

The concept of *capacity* refers to both the experience and the skills of the members of the department in responding to change. Thus capacity sensitizes us to the institutional competence of the members, the skills, knowledge, contacts and experience they can draw upon. Such competence might seek to support and sustain 'readerly' interpretations of the intended and actual facets of policy or be more 'writerly', critical and oppositional. The leadership styles (Knip and Van der Vegt 1991) of the senior teachers and heads of department are also significant here.

Contingencies

This draws our attention to the factors which may advance or inhibit the possibilities of change – staffing (recruitment, experience, specialization), student recruitment, inherited plant and facilities, etc. Clearly these two concepts overlap and remain crucially affected by other aspects of policy. However, we would suggest they help us to recognize powerful contextual factors in schools' and departments' responses to change.

Commitments and histories

In a similar sense commitment and history are often closely connected. The former refers to the existence of firmly held and well entrenched subject or pedagogical paradigms within a department (or school). The latter refers to what Knip and Van der Vegt (1991) call the *innovation histories* of schools or departments. That is the existence (or not) of a history of curriculum development and change. A history of curriculum change can reduce the threat involved in the possibility of further change but it is also typically associated with high levels of commitment.

We do have evidence that low capacity, low commitment and no history of innovation results in a high degree of reliance upon policy texts, external direction and advice, which in some circumstances verges on panic or leads to high uncertainty and confusion and a sense of threat. Equally we have evidence that high capacity, high commitment and a history of innovation may provide a basis for a greater sense of autonomy and writerliness with regard to policy texts, a greater willingness to interpret texts in the light of previous practice, and a greater likelihood therefore of 'reconciliation' and 'mutation' (Corwin 1983).

This leads us to suggest that the differential impacts of contingencies, institutional structures, cultures, histories and environments may produce very different kinds of possibilities of response. For teachers these features make up part of the 'operational terrain' within which policies are 'implemented'. But, as we have noted, in the National Curriculum policy the assumption is made that schools operate and will respond in terms of *ideal* conditions for change. Hence there is the assumption of commonality, even sameness, among schools, that all are equally able to respond, equally prepared, equally resourced. That is clearly wrong. Furthermore, the basis of differences between schools in not just a matter of resources or of the skills and experience of key participants, no matter how important those things are. It is also a matter of differences in the interpretations of key texts; Knip and Van der Vegt (1991) call this 'translation'. To put it another way, the authors of the National Curriculum are limited in their capacity to control the meanings embedded in the texts. As a result such texts are read and appreciated differently in different settings.

The four schools in this study have markedly different catchment areas and student populations. The mix of major institutional concerns although basically similar overall were balanced differently in each case. In part, this balance was also reflected in the institutional histories and the work cultures of their staffs (gender was a factor in this). The substance and conceptualization of institutional leadership was different in each case and the attendant micro-political tussles were inflected differently. Some of the schools had a history of innovation which meant that they were better placed to engage with further innovation but also wary about not losing the benefits of previous developments, to which they were committed. All of these factors affect and constitute particular readings of the policy texts and provide what Knip and Van der Vegt (1991) call 'scenarios for change'. 'A scenario reflects the response of the social system to the policy intervention and as such indicates the degree to which the school actually allows the central policy to enter its system' (p.125). Further, according to Knip and Van der Vegt the scenario for change in a particular institution can be thought of: 'as an outcome of a process of *self-reflection* in the school provoked by the policy intervention. Attention then shifts from the organization as an adapting system to the organization as a *self-producing system*' (p.129).

Thus, we are arguing that change in the school is best understood in terms of a complex interplay between the history, culture and context of the school and the intentions and requirements of the producers of policy texts. This interplay cannot be reduced to adaptation or 'successive approximation' (Eveland *et al*. 1977), rather it is a process of 'mutation' (Corwin 1983). Similar variations, to those in the schools, can be identified between different subject departments. In terms of rough generalization it is even possible to talk about different 'interpretational stances' in different departments. In some cases, the interpretation of texts is proactive, critical and self-assured, what Barthes (Hawkes 1977) might call 'writerly'. We might also want to call this a 'professional' response in the sense that it preserves a strong role for the teachers. In others, the interpretations have been more reactive, passive and unquestioning, what Barthes might call 'readerly'. We might want to call this a 'technician' response, in that the National Curriculum texts are read like technical, 'how-to-do-it' manuals rather than as professional documents.

Our concluding point then, is that as policy the National Curriculum remains both the object and subject of struggles over meaning. It is not so much being 'implemented' in schools as being 're-created', not so much 'reproduced' as 'produced'. While schools are changing as a result, so too is the National Curriculum. This leaves us with a strong feeling that the state control model is analytically very limited. Our empirical data do not suggest that the State is *without* power. But, equally it indicates such power is strongly circumscribed by the contextual features of institutions, over which the State may find that control is both problematic and contradictory in terms of other political projects.

Chapter 5

Special Educational Needs in a new context

> It has taken nearly a century of compulsory school attendance for the education of children with special needs to capture a small sector of the political high ground in education and for new policies reducing segregation and categorization to begin to be implemented. Its precarious hold on that high ground and the future of the new policies now appear even more vulnerable in the face of the new Education Reform Act.
>
> (Heward and Lloyd-Smith 1990, p.34)

Heward and Lloyd-Smith are referring here to the very different effects of the Warnock Report (1978), the Education Act 1981 and the Education Reform Act 1988. The Report of the Committee of Inquiry into the Education of Handicapped Children and Young People, chaired by Mary Warnock, was the first 'official' application of the language of social justice to this marginalized group of people. The Warnock Committee recommended a radical re-thinking of the educational provision for children and young people with special educational needs. In particular the abolition of the categories of handicap, in an effort to remove the labelling which often operated to keep children in special schools and the widening of the definition of special educational needs to apply to a much larger group of children. The committee suggested that this was necessary in order to plan services for special educational provision which could properly address the learning difficulties of up to 20 per cent of children, at some time during their school careers. But almost more important, they challenged the language of description for special education: away from the deficit mode, to a conception of the whole person. For example, the committee recommended that children who were previously described as 'remedial' or 'educationally subnormal' should instead be described as 'children with learning difficulties'; they introduced a language that brought with it expectations of excellence, such as 'educational opportunities of quality'. Warnock was the first 'official' policy text to challenge the 'otherness' of special education provision.

The Education Act 1981 was greatly influenced by the Warnock Report, and continued with the same discourse of planning to meet special educational needs in the mainstream of the education system. It attempted to legitimate this philosophy within a legislative framework. Furthermore, given the pressures that had led to Warnock it was not altogether suprising that the Education Act 1981 provided the stimulus for a massive outpouring of literature and research relating special needs to mainstream provision. Special Educational Needs (SEN) has become a key component of teacher education courses both pre- and in-service. However, as Heward and Lloyd-Smith suggest, it may be that Warnock did no more than provide a short interregnum between periods within which different forms of marginalization held sway.

SPECIAL EDUCATIONAL NEEDS PROVISION IN THE 1990s

The Education Reform Act, and specifically national testing and the National Curriculum threaten a new kind of exclusion for children with special educational needs. At first glance, the language of the Act is still recognizably influenced by Warnock. It claims to enshrine notions of access to a 'balanced and broadly based curriculum', and requires that those children with special educational needs who require exemption from parts of the National Curriculum should have that exemption examined every six months. This would appear to ensure that educationists are reminded of the entitlement of students with special educational needs to the full curriculum, and seems to seek to keep those students in sight if they are exempted from the curriculum. However, as with the Education Act 1981, local authorities, and even more, individual schools, will continue to give their own interpretation to the provision of SEN within the Education Reform Act. Not only through their own ideological positions about social justice and their definitions of appropriate provision for special needs, but also in terms of their particular institutional priorities. While some common ground has been established there remain wide variations in practice and levels of provision. Heward and Lloyd-Smith (1990), assessing the impact of legislation on special education policy, see threats in the 1988 Act to even the common ground:

> Bringing this powerless and politically unattractive minority [those with learning difficulties] into closer relations with the mainstream after such a lengthy period of rigid categorization and segregation was a difficult task requiring considerable commitment and resources, neither of which has been evident in the 1981 Act and its implementation. Consequently, following the pattern of all earlier legislation in special education, implementation has varied widely among schools and local authorities. The [Education Reform] Act is a development which threatens the new directions of special education policy and may reinstate the former assumptions with greater force.
>
> (p.21)

Most significantly, the ERA places provision for SEN within a budgetary and a market context as well as a curricular and assessment framework. SEN provisions in school will have to be weighed and justified against other forms of staffing and expenditure. Arguments about good practice have now to be viewed in terms of opportunity costs. How will those schools which have decided to take on whole school special needs policies maintain that commitment, and keep the department and policy central to the school? With the new systems of teacher pay being developed, linking pay to matters of appraisal and 'merit', with massive shortages in some subjects (Association for Science Education *et al.* 1991) how will they justify paying SEN key teachers allowances? Outside the school in the education marketplace, will the presence of children with special educational needs attract new pupils? Will schools decide not to have any pupils with special educational needs if their presence affects enrolment? It remains to be seen whether market forces make philosophies about whole-school provision for children with special educational needs either too expensive or too problematic.

We are concerned here with the provision for students with special educational needs within mainstream secondary schools. This means that we are addressing the needs of perhaps 19 of

Warnock's 20 per cent, the majority without Statements of Special Educational Need, some with Statements, but all in mainstream schools. In the current educational and political climate, meeting these needs in mainstream schools seems to throw up a number of tensions and dilemmas which we want to explore in the remainder of this chapter.

SPECIAL EDUCATIONAL NEEDS AND THE NATIONAL CURRICULUM

The idea of a National Curriculum has, we suggest, a highly complex and problematic relationship to the issue of SEN provision in schools, and to the educational experiences of students defined as having special educational needs. Rendered into crude and simple terms, the point is whether the National Curriculum will be viewed as a mechanism for ensuring a set of common educational experiences for all students, including those with special educational needs – a decisive break from the deficit curriculum previously experienced by many students with special educational needs – or as a set of constraints and limits which will inhibit teachers to such an extent that the individual needs of students with special educational needs will be either ignored altogether, or will remain an unattainable ideal within the realities and demands of the National Curriculum classroom. The National Curriculum Council (NCC 1989) in their document *A Curriculum for All*, certainly set high standards for teachers. A whole new set of demands on the teachers' time, skills and commitments are 'added on' to their existing classroom tasks. They define a 'good learning environment' for students with special educational needs as including: '. . . an atmosphere of encouragement, acceptance, respect for achievements and sensitivity to individual needs, in which all pupils can thrive' (p.7); and go on to argue that:

> Curriculum development plans, schemes of work, and classroom and school environments need to be closely aligned with the teaching needs and individual curriculum plans of pupils with learning difficulties and disabilities so that maximum access to the National Curriculum is ensured.
>
> (p.7)

David Galloway (1990) among others takes a positive and

optimistic view of this sort of educational rhetoric and the values it espouses. He argues that: 'the National Curriculum, national testing and provision for grant-maintained status may all be seen to have *potential* [our emphasis] benefits for pupils with Special Educational Needs' (p.51). Indeed he goes on to suggest that: '. . . although the GERBIL [Great Education Reform Bill, i.e., the 1988 Act] is in fact the product of a reforming right wing government, an identical bill might equally well have been produced by a reforming government dominated by Marxists' (p.51). As regards the National Curriculum specifically, Galloway's key point is that the imposition of a legislative minimum curriculum for all children can go a long way towards ensuring that students with special educational needs are not disadvantaged by the forms of curriculum exclusion which currently operate in many schools: '. . . an alternative low-status curriculum that restricts rather than enhances their opportunities . . . where proliferation of options is used to shunt pupils of below average ability into a non-examination siding' (p.58). Thus, he asserts: 'The requirement that all pupils should have access to the full range of the National Curriculum may make it more difficult for schools to marginalize their pupils with special needs' (p.58).

However, Galloway's notion of the National Curriculum as a panacea for special educational needs totally ignores the question of 'whose' curriculum is being nationalized. The National Curriculum is a particular selection from national culture, as Ken Jones (1979) is at pains to point out. It cannot be assumed that the National Curriculum will engage with or reflect the interests of students with special educational needs. Nonetheless, on the face of it, Galloway has a point. Indeed the National Curriculum can be seen as a step towards a more comprehensive national education system. But, whatever its *potential* benefits the National Curriculum as realized in the 'context of practice' must be examined carefully and critically. Although Galloway is dismissive of criticisms of the National Curriculum as so much professional special pleading, there must be real doubts about whether the mix of common provision with sensitivity to individual needs, set in the context of national testing, is actually feasible and realizable in the 25–35 pupil comprehensive school classroom. It may equally well be the case that the National Curriculum becomes a set of constraints on good SEN practice which makes it increasingly difficult to achieve that sensitivity to individual needs.

Too much may be expected of teachers given current levels of, or even reducing levels of, resources and support. Thus, another recent writer on SEN (Ramasut 1989) takes exactly the opposite position to that of Galloway.

It is clear that without amendments to the Education Reform Act, the education of a large minority of pupils will be put in jeopardy. A whole-school approach to meeting special needs [which we discuss later in the chapter] could be made more difficult to achieve.

(p.18)

Our point then is that the relationship of the Education Reform Act and the National Curriculum in particular to SEN depends not so much on the potential benefits of an inclusive common curriculum, as on the context of constraints and possibilities within which such needs are catered for and responded to in the classroom and in the schools. We would suggest, somewhat bluntly, that too much is being asked of teachers. The National Curriculum, as it stands, is fixed, heavily prescribed and rests on a strongly normative model of progress in learning. The system of national testing carries with it a presupposition of classroom, institutional and area comparisons. It is difficult to see comparisons not being made also within schools (between teachers) and within classrooms (between students). (Especially if schemes like the one proposed by the London Borough of Wandsworth, for keeping poor performers down a year, become more common). The National Curriculum provides a potential for a language of hierarchy and comparison based on levels of achievement. Against all this the teacher must provide flexibility, differential pacing, individual classroom support, encouragement and reinforcement. But if problems arise what will be blamed first – the teacher or the National Curriculum?

Perhaps like so many other writers on SEN Galloway makes good educational practice sound too easy. So much of the 'success' of the National Curriculum rides on the skills, goodwill and perhaps guilt and commitment of well-intentioned teachers. Too little attention is given to the practical, financial, market – and micro-political factors which may serve to inhibit good practice, but which are also a part of the organizational infrastructure imposed on schools by the Education Reform Act. Thus, the question of SEN and 'education for all' ultimately rests within practice and school provision. How can and will SEN be handled in schools in the new ERA? The relationship of SEN provision to the National Curriculum and curriculum development may not always be clear in practice.

> A lot of departments, I know the maths department, already they've been beavering away. Last term they had each taken a year group and tried to rewrite a scheme of work and rewrite the syllabus in the light of the National Curriculum, and writing attainment targets and tests and things, and science I think are doing the same. So everybody is doing it but I'm not around. I'm not involved in it yet and at the moment I find it very difficult to see where I'm going to fit in.
>
> (Head of SEN, Parkside, 12 February 1990)

In relation to other processes and expectations SEN may be an afterthought.

THE CONTEXT OF PRACTICE: THE NATIONAL CURRICULUM

In her review of the NCC booklet, 'A curriculum for all: special educational needs in the National Curriculum', Pound (1990) refers to what she sees as the worrying failure to tackle the issues of disapplication and the extent to which this might undermine the principle of entitlement for all, and the linked matter of the suitability of the National Curriculum for students with special educational needs. She further points out that:

> Practitioners may also be dismayed by the omission of any discussion of the impacts of (a) new procedures for assessing children and for publishing results, (b) open enrolment procedures and (c) local financial management, on provision for pupils with special educational needs. (p.112)

Understandably, in what is a short review she has no opportunity to explore these issues in any detail. We therefore want to examine some of the new contexts that may affect the development of whole-school policies for SEN. Drawing upon the work of Bernstein we would suggest the intended structure of the National Curriculum, its subject basis and the process of introduction imply a strong classification and framing (Bernstein, 1975). The Attainment Targets and Programmes of Study in the

Statutory Orders issued for mathematics, science, English, technology, geography and history carry within them varying degrees of prescriptiveness. However, overall there are clear distinctions being drawn between subject boundaries and, on the surface, the basis of knowledge is carefully compartmentalized (see Chapter 4). Teachers and students have much more limited control than previously over what is taught and the pace of teaching. This crucially affects the organization of the learning process. While the non-statutory orders and the appeal to consider cross-curricular links indicate a recognition that such rigidity may not be educationally appropriate, it may be some years before this strong classification can be readily broken down. In the case of framing, teachers face the pressure of SATs, testing and the publishing of results in deciding how much they try to teach to individual students and the pace at which they do so. Thus, in terms of the prescriptiveness of the content, the structure of the curriculum and the pace of the teaching, the National Curriculum may seriously undermine the sort of flexibility teachers will require to in order to respond to student needs and especially to special educational needs. In simple terms, teachers may find themselves responding to the needs of the curriculum and assessment rather than to the students' individual needs. Some of the flavour of this is apparent in the following comment from the Head of the SEN department at Parkside about the possible impact of the National Curriculum and assessment:

> The problem I feel is that departments will turn round to me and say well I don't want that child to go [out for SEN withdrawal] because they're going to miss out on doing a piece of work that's leading up to an attainment target and I don't want them to miss it . . .
>
> (HOD, SEN, Parkside, 12 February 1990)

This needs to be contrasted with the positive view that the differentiation set up by the National Curriculum has actually led some teachers to question the whole-class approach. The Head of Special Educational Needs clearly felt that this had given her a greater opportunity to promote SEN provision with other staff:

> Most staff, in reading their documents, are quite concerned that children have to achieve these different levels of

attainment, and they're beginning to realize that there are
children within their class with a varied level of attainment . . .
and how are they going to provide for that?

(HOD, SEN, Parkside, 6 April 1990)

This raises the question of whether good practice in relation to
SEN can exist within the parameters of the Education Reform
Act. For example, is there a contradiction between whole-school
SEN provision and the demands of the National Curriculum? A
whole-school policy is built on the assumption that 'education for
all' implies that all children will learn the different parts of the
agreed curriculum from subject specialists. This model has been
taking shape at Parkside School, the SEN department has
emerged from the Portakabin in the playground, where it housed
one full-time teacher and several others filling in 18 periods a
week, to develop a whole school structure of key teachers
working to the SEN teacher. The previously marginalized department has been centralized, and all the staff of the school are being
encouraged and supported in their integration of students with
special needs.

Around the National Curriculum core, the school-based SEN
teachers act as a resource to the subject teachers, ensuring that
subject matter and the teaching materials are accessible to students with learning difficulties. The SEN teachers offer a professional package to subject teachers that may include notions of
differentiation, an ability to explore methods of recording
learning other than by writing, and an examination of methods of
pedagogy so that different routes of learning are acknowledged.
Subject teachers are gradually enabled to co-ordinate the planning for children with special educational needs in their lessons
with support from three sources. One source is the school SEN
department who will offer advice on methods of learning and
diagnoses of the particular learning difficulties of the children in
the lessons. Another source is the key post-holder within the
subject areas. These are teachers on their first allowance, usually
an 'A', whose role is to remind the subject department of the
presence of children with special needs in their lessons and to
explore subject-based materials. At Parkside, the Head of the SEN
Department tries to gather the key teachers together regularly for
meetings to discuss their work. These meetings are a form of staff
development, as the key teachers have expressed interest in

working with such children, but usually have not received any training to do so:

> At the first meeting this term I asked them to draw up a checklist, subject-specific, the idea being that if a teacher in their department was concerned about a child they will go to the key teacher, about things that could be done within the department, to try to iron out some of the difficulties.
> (HOD, SEN, Parkside, 23 November 1990)

One problem with the key teacher scheme is that these teachers are often those who are most effective and mobile and who apply for and get promotion. They do not stay within the key teacher scheme very long. At Parkside, two terms after the introduction of the scheme, the Head of the SEN Department was working with two replacements within her team of five key teachers. However, if the promotion is within the school, and if their replacements are also from within the school, many more teachers will have had the opportunity to take responsibility for developing strategies to support the subject-based learning of children with special needs:

> I think it's kind of doing it through the back door method, but I think in a way I'm doing it sort of the right way, I think. I think if I confronted the whole staff head on and said we've got to do this, there would be resistance, but I'm niggling away.
> (HOD, SEN, Parkside, 23 November 1990)

The third source of support for subject teachers would be the in-class presence of support teachers provided by Statements of Special Educational Need for those children who have been through the assessment and statementing procedure.

THE CONTEXT OF PRACTICE: LMS AND THE LEAs

However, in important respects it may not be the National Curriculum that will have the major impact upon SEN provision. LMS and its impact upon the relationship of schools to LEAs, upon the internal dynamics of the school and upon the new relationship of schools to the outside world in the form of educational 'market forces', could well prove far more pervasive. In the case of schools and their LEAs there are important respects in which individual school policies on SEN provision may be

restricted and limited by the new relationship resulting from the
ERA. The first hinges upon developments that relate to local
authority funding in general, namely, the politics of the poll tax
(or whatever system replaces it) and the Government's decision
to carry out 'capping' on various authorities. Although cuts in
LEA funding from central Government have usually had some
consequences for educational expenditure, the use of a 'formula'
(for the allocation of funding to individual schools) means that
budget items are preset by agreement with the DES (see below).
The fact that the government has also retained the option to
extend their powers with respect to capping means that
individual school budgets may well become dependent upon
'politics' that the school is unable to control. The outcome seems
likely to make SEN provision open to the vagaries of both LEA
expenditure levels and within that the levels that the formula
provides. In both cases this could seriously limit the flexibility a
school would be able to exercise in providing for students with
special educational needs. Of course the higher the proportion of
the LEA budget schools are allocated on a per capita basis, the
less fine-tuning there is possible in producing different funding
to schools for SEN and the more freedom for manoeuvre individual schools have in determining the balance between needs
and expenditure. (A number of authorities already have schemes
which allocate more than the 1990 minimum of 75 per cent of the
school budget via pupil numbers, most LEAs are required to
allocate 85 per cent by 1993, Kent already operates at the 85 per
cent level and 13 other LEAs set their figure above the 75 per cent
minimum.) Some LEAs are already clearly concerned that too
many statements for SEN children will put too much drain in
their overall schools budget. Westway is a case in point:

> the LEA's delaying on these, they're just putting the blocks on
> it because too many children are being statemented, and what
> with cuts and everything, they're trying to cut back. They're
> even talking now of reducing it from £2,000 per head to £1,000
> per head. The Head said that the LEA told the heads that, I
> think over the next two years, there has to be an 8 per cent cut
> in the education budget.
>
> (HOD, SEN, Parkside, 13 July 1990)

The statementing of SEN students under the provisions of the
Education Act also 1981 raises budgetary issues. The more

statements completed, the more the cost of support provision required from the LEA. Furthermore, the requirement to devolve expenditures of various sorts from LEAs to schools may also mean the loss of important aspects of the LEA's strategic role in 'orchestrating a complex range of services in meeting individual special needs' (Russell 1990, p.207). The use of devolved monies now rests with school governors, and again as Russell points out: '... the new generation of parent governor-managers may have a sharper view of what constitutes quality in education and the optimum targets for their budgets in order to achieve such goals' (p.216). There is also the fact that the formula is applied across the LEA. While under LMS schools are expected to control their own budgets and to make their own decisions (in this case, expenditure on SEN provision as against other expenditure), the distribution of monies to the schools is done according to a 'formula', which is developed by the LEA and must meet with DES approval. LEAs are not required to follow any particular model of consultation with the schools over this formula and our research indicates the degree and forms of consultation vary considerably. Few authorities appear to have involved the schools wholeheartedly in developing the formula, although the government-imposed pressure of tight timing has been more important here than an LEA commitment to exclude schools. A 'typical' process of 'consultation' has been to issue a series of possible formulas and ask schools to respond, individually, to the impact of each successive formula. This has minimized the opportunity schools have had to compare how far 'needs' and elements of the formula correspond across schools and has maximized the pursuit of short-term, individual financial considerations. Thus, schools have looked at and responded in terms of their 'needs' in isolation and as they currently stand. In Westway LEA this process led to the demise of a number of centrally funded services – for example the Reading Centre. Schools which did not make much use of the Centre wanted the costs devolved to them; those schools which made extensive use of the Centre could no longer afford to support its work via 'buying-in' for services rendered. The Centre closed, children with learning difficulties lost support and an effective redistribution of resources to schools with lesser need took place. Once the formula is fixed, schools are only able to negotiate with the authorities for funding on that basis. Consequently SEN provision in schools starts from the formula and not from the needs of the student. The categorization of the needs of the student population according to criteria laid down in the formula becomes a technical matter. This replaces the exercise of professional judgement. The formula is a clear but blunt instrument.

Westway LEA distributed a circular to schools explaining the LMS funding for pupils with special educational needs. It proposed that pupils with Statements of Special Educational Needs will be funded according to their needs at one of five levels, ranging from £2,268 for students with category A needs (moderate learning difficulties, specific learning difficulties including dyslexic difficulties, general learning difficulties, visual impairment and pupils in developmental/diagnostic placements), to £6,804 for students with category E needs (hearing impaired, severe learning difficulties, secondary deaf/blind). The Head of SEN at Parkside commented:

> The Deputy Head in charge of finances asked me whether I could get more children statemented so that we could get more money for the school.
>
> (HOD, SEN, Parkside, 13 July 1990)

Students and their needs are increasingly viewed primarily in financial terms, rather than in terms of individual need. The financial allocation determines response. And the question of what students are worth has also been raised rather differently in the school setting. While statemented students may well have quite high 'price tags', the remaining 18 per cent could be seen to be something of a liability (see also Chapter 2)

> You are caught . . . and this is where LMS really raises its ugly head, in terms of true educational things. Each child has a price tag on it, and the sixth formers have the highest price tag, so in pure financial terms one obviously is trying to raise the most amount of money you can. But Flightpath staff have always been conscious of our intake being skewed towards the less able child, and through the years we have developed what has got to be considered one of the best supportive education departments in the Borough. But of course the less able children tend not to stay on to the sixth form, unless we feel they are really going to benefit from it, and we have an excellent record, through our guidance department, of ensuring that our

children get into employment as well. So you have this conflict
of trying to ensure you've got a big sixth form, trying to ensure
that you are really doing the best for the individual child, and
the introduction of the disabled children. I don't think that's a
sort of problem for us in terms of whether it was a bad image
or not. I mean I think personally it can do nothing but good for
us but one has got to recognize the fact that these children do
take a lot of extra time.

(Senior teacher, Flightpath, 23 March 1990)

Schools are thus faced with some genuine dilemmas. Do they
promote SEN provision in order to attract statemented students
with a 'high' worth and then risk gaining an 'image' locally as a
low ability school, or try to attract high ability students who will
stay on and enhance the school's reputation academically? And
what about those students who fall into the less well-funded 18
per cent? Such dilemmas are apparent in the following comment:

I've done quite a bit in terms of promoting special needs, for
example, because I think we've got more than average special
needs in the area that we're serving, so I think that's something
that we ought to say is part of our wares. Other people have
said to me, 'if you keep advertising special needs, you will turn
away brighter kids'. And maybe there's an element of that, but
you have to recognize that you are a servant of a particular
area and not try to kid yourself that you're going to become a
different type of school if only you could market yourself
better.

(Senior Deputy, Flightpath, 6 July 1989)

A great deal here is going to depend upon the gaps between the
worth of different students and their availability in the local area
as well as the marketing decisions schools might make. Consequently the degree to which schools respond to the special needs
of individual students is going to be affected by financial
decisions (balancing the budget at LEA and school levels), local
demography and the vagaries of the 'market', all of which are
only marginally within SEN teachers' control.

Within the schools, deciding how the school budget will be
spent places SEN provision into an arena of struggle and negoti-
ation that appears on the surface to be about finances. In fact
questions of personal status, protecting or promoting 'subject'

positions and educational ideologies are all part of the powerful sub-text. The Head of the SEN department at Parkside was clearly aware of this in relation to her own, and thus, to her specialism's status:

> And the schools I went to where people were on a C or a D and they were included in the senior management team, were fantastic, 'cos they had a real input and a real say and people listened to them. Whereas here I'm just a Department Head, I'm not a policy maker. I think the B just reflects the level of importance.
>
> (HOD, SEN, Parkside, 12 February 1990)

While the HOD had the 'ear' of the headteacher, it remained apparent that she was, in her words, 'not a policy maker'. In the longer term, what is spent on SEN provision will have to be argued against textbooks for a core subject area, or decoration of the entrance hall to enhance the market appeal of the school, or employing a further teacher to decrease class sizes for a practical subject. Access to or exclusion from the main sites of decision-making and policy formulation will continue to be crucial. At this stage the teacher feels very aware of the pressures and constraints of the budget, but can do little more than lobby those who hold the purse strings:

> I think budgeting and everything is so tight that I can go and demand till I'm blue in the face really for a qualified assistant, full-time, but realistically I'm not going to get it, so you've got to work with what you've got.
>
> (HOD, SEN, Parkside, 1 November 1989)

Both financial and educational issues have to be argued within a shifting power structure which may or may not privilege the position of SEN provision within the school (see Chapter 6). It seems clear that a headteacher's personal educational ideology around SEN provision can be a particularly powerful influence on decision-making about the resourcing and positioning of the SEN department. The headteacher at Parkside explained his thinking behind centralizing the SEN department and developing a whole school policy for SEN provision:

> You do things because you have an agenda yourself, and priorities within that agenda, but the good thing about the

National Curriculum is that it has highlighted certain areas to make people generally more aware. Special needs have come in out of the cold. So if one of the questions you're asking is 'did I have a master plan really?' Then the answer to that would be, only insofar as it was one of the issues which I was very firmly determined, of which I was *very* determined on dealing with through the curriculum, rather than in any side issues.

(Head, Parkside, 6 April 1990)

Here the headteacher is the critical reality definer (Riseborough 1981), using such language as 'agenda','priorities', 'very firmly determined' to describe his commitment to a whole-school special needs policy. The political patronage he exercises with respect to SEN has led to significant changes. Maintaining, preserving and extending those changes presently revolves around the continued commitment of the Head and the work of the Head of the SEN department. However, policy networks in schools vary considerably.

Flightpath School, also in Westway LEA, has an SEN department of eight full-time teachers, many of them with relevant qualifications, and a head of department who attends meetings of the School Management Committee (SMC). Their provision is based on whole SEN classes, reminiscent in this respect of remedial classes, with subjects such as mathematics, English and humanities taught by SEN teachers, and students withdrawn from other subjects for their special needs support. The size of the department and the presence of the head of department on the SMC suggests a high level of commitment to special needs, a fact the other members of the department recognize:

She's involved in senior management, so I've been lucky. What's been relevant has been discussed. We have access to information fairly quickly and she's good at telling us things we ought to know. So at that level we have more awareness than most people.

(Main grade SEN teacher, Flightpath, 28 September 1990)

But the apparently strong strategic position of the head of department has still not been enough to ward off 'cuts'. Thus the following policy decision was reported to the June, 1990 Governors' Meeting:

One casualty of cuts has been the loss of in-class support for SEN, it's now all withdrawal and that's the best we can do within the financial constraints.

(Senior teacher, Flightpath, 21 June 1990)

The head of the SEN department reflecting upon the decision, at a later date, observed:

It's because of LMS the class size is going up.

(HOD, SEN, Flightpath, 20 July 1990)

Protecting the interests of SEN in the school required not only arguing her case against other departmental interests but also against the global financial concerns of the senior management for the whole school. The insertion of the 'financial' into the 'educational' can impose profound limits on ways of thinking about SEN provision.

I just worry about whether what we do, whether we couldn't do it differently and do it more effectively. But my worry is that I know whoever I talk to on the senior management, will also confirm what I say, that if we didn't stand up in front of classes and teach classes, then I wouldn't have a department, no matter how many arguments I put forward, no matter how many statemented children.

(HOD, SEN, Flightpath, 20 July 1990)

Thus the introduction of LMS provides a new and powerful stimulus for micro-political struggle around SEN provision. Financial priorities confront interpretations of good SEN practice very directly. The history of commitments to SEN work and the status and role of the head of SEN will certainly affect future planning. For students identified as having learning difficulties, SEN provision can, under the system of LMS funding, attract additional monies. But schools are aware that there may be longer-term costs involved in giving too high a profile to SEN work; market image, national testing performance and staying-on rates in the sixth form may conspire to produce new kinds of exclusion or marginalization for SEN students. Schools will face ethical dilemmas which set professional commitments against financial expediency.

CONCLUSION

If, as suggested here, the achievement of 'Education for All' is best translated into a whole-school special needs policy, then within the provisions of the Education Reform Act, the effectiveness of such a policy *depends* on financial and micro-political struggles over the various constraints and possibilities mapped out in Figure 5.1.

Effectiveness depends on the constraints or possibilities imposed or opened up by the National Curriculum and the attendant testing, attainment targets and published results, and the consequent development of differentiated work. It depends on

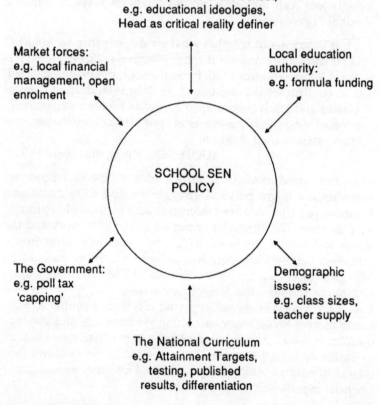

The micro-politics of the school,
e.g. educational ideologies,
Head as critical reality definer

Market forces:
e.g. local financial
management, open
enrolment

Local education
authority:
e.g. formula funding

SCHOOL SEN
POLICY

The Government:
e.g. poll tax
'capping'

Demographic
issues:
e.g. class sizes,
teacher supply

The National Curriculum
e.g. Attainment Targets,
testing, published
results, differentiation

Figure 5.1   The constraints and possibilities which could affect a school's SEN provision.

government-imposed poll tax 'capping' which is different in different authorities, and thus allows some LEAs to spend more on education than others. It depends on the resources available to schools, both demographically as in class sizes and teacher supply, and as a result of the LEAs' formula funding. It depends on how much money statemented students and non-statemented students with special educational needs bring with them. It depends on market forces, and whether schools under local financial management and Open Enrolment will find that their whole-school SEN policies will make them more or less attractive to potential customers. And it depends on the micro-politics of the school: the educational ideology and the value systems of the headteacher, and of the governors, of the head of the SEN department, and the access of SEN advocates to influence over school policy making and financial allocations.

Chapter 6

Changing management and the management of change!

> The graveyards of history are strewn with the corpses of reformers who failed utterly to reform anything . . . men and women who failed not only because of the forces arrayed against them, but because the pictures in their minds about power and influence were simplistic and inaccurate.
>
> (Dahl 1970)

In this chapter we want to consider, in more detail, the implications for management of the *complexity* of change in schools brought about, in part, by the very varied requirements and provisions of the Act. While our particular concern is with how schools 'manage' this complexity it is equally apparent that management itself has been targeted for reform. In the Act the 'agents of change' in schools, for the most part Heads and the senior management team, are also seen as 'objects of change' with respect to their culture and practices. In particular, they are being encouraged to be more self-determining, entrepreneurial, cost-effective and consumer orientated (see Chapter 3). This duality has considerable implications for the management of change in schools that go beyond handling an expanded set of demands and which involve a reconsideration of the purposes of management in schools. While this kind of reorientation is not new, either to schools or in other organizations, the conception of the social market within the Act sets new 'ground rules' for the management of schools. Our intention is not to evaluate the viability of different management models for the 'new times' schools now face. Instead we want to draw out some of the dilemmas and contradictions that school managers now confront. This involves looking at the management of change in practice and thus, necessarily, at the changing of management. We want to begin, however, by making two general points about the pro-cesses of educational change.

Many studies of educational change, and certainly some attempts to report on the implementation of the ERA, have tended to reproduce two dire flaws in their conceptualization of change – as Dahl (1970) puts it the 'pictures in the minds' of the researchers are 'simplistic and inaccurate'. The first of these flaws is the single change focus. That is, the often unexplained assumption that one facet of change – the National Curriculum, LMS, assessment, teachers' pedagogies – can be addressed in isolation, almost as though the other provisions of the Act did not exist or do not impinge (see Bolam 1982, Wallace 1990). Yet change in institutions is rarely uni-dimensional and the ERA certainly cannot be viewed as a series of parallel but only weakly interrelated innovations (see Wallace 1988 on innovation and sub-innovation, Wallace 1990 on dimensions of variation between innovations). LMS, the National Curriculum, Records of Achievement and Standard Assessment Tasks have different pedigrees and carry different sorts of ideological baggage, but their interrelations and the effects in and on schools must be seen in composite and holistic terms.

The second flaw is the neglect of institutional history. The assumption, again often unexplained, is that life begins with the moment of innovation, rather than seeing new changes as related to and building upon a history of old ones. Change is set within and is accommodated to the micro-political history of the institution. Furthermore the history of change in institutions is typically a history of conflict, it is rarely the technical and consensual process that so many organizational theorists portray.

Change in schools is rarely politically neutral. Interests are enhanced or threatened by change. 'Conflict and change are inevitably interlocked as any redistribution of power and privilege will be sought by some and resisted by others' (Kelly 1969, p.69). Furthermore, change does not usually arise within a set of social relationships which have been previously untouched by competition or dissension. Advocates and opponents typically 'dig in' along established lines of ideological dispute.

(Ball 1987, p.78)

We would add that in the case of the ERA, there is a deliberate empowering of certain individuals and groups over others. It is as much about the redistribution of powers and priviledges *within* institutions as it is about redistribution *between* them. The relationships between schools and the market, schools and the LEA and DES have changed but so have the relationships between teachers and school managers. However, while we are focusing on what Heidegger refers to as the move from the 'no longer' to the 'not yet' we do not want to fall into the easy but misguided assumption that any innovation is the same in every institution, that the 'reality' of the innovation is clear and unequivocal; that there is only one 'real'. Rather, we suggest, innovations are interpreted and responded to on the basis of the divergent 'interests' and the perspectives of different organizational members. The new possibilities for changing power relations and securing privileges, embedded within the innovations themselves, are resources for the micro-political struggles that go on within the institutions.

There is a second aspect to the relation between history and innovation. For there is a history of innovations in schools that stretches far back beyond the ERA. That history cannot be swept away. It is not a simple matter of 'off with the old and on with the new'. Schools develop an ethos and a culture, practices become routinized, commitments embedded and beliefs and meanings accumulate in fairly unplanned and often diverse ways. As a deputy head at Flightpath put it, talking about developing the School Management Plan:

> So I mean it was a question of, it's like going into a messy room and tidying it up, that was the job we were doing. Not deciding whether we ought to have the things we had in that room, or some others it was like just for goodness sake let's just get it into some form of order so that when they ask us the questions, we can say, ah well that's there and that's there, that's what we're going to do for the next two or three years.

Schools cannot start with a 'clean slate'. Tidying up the room reveals unseen messes. Existing piles and files no longer serve the new purposes. Change does not enter into a new room but one that has been ordered for the purposes of the inhabitants. In other words institutional practices have to be challenged and changed. But it also needs to be said that any analysis of change in school management should not rest on a kind of 'golden ageism'. We are not suggesting the effect of the ERA has been to destroy something perfect or wonderful in the way schools used to be run. Indeed, many of the aspects of the move to what we call 'new management' were already in train prior to the Act. Hellawell (1990), for example, argues that it was the teachers' industrial action during 1984–7 that produced a point of break from previous practice. He says, 'The "critical incidents" produced by the dispute have, in some cases, made both school staffs and heads analyse the nature of their previous relationships and made them question whether the latter are still workable' (p. 401); and 'What I think my interviews suggest is that in some schools in the UK the Government-imposed settlement has made staffs see heads less as fellow professionals and more as line managers' (p.403). The ERA may well have enhanced such changes, or at least made it more difficult to defend and preserve the 'old' practices.

'NEW MANAGEMENT', NEW CONCERNS AND NEW DILEMMAS

The extent of the complexity we have found in our case-study schools produces considerable difficulty in assembling a sensible and concise account and to achieve this we have resorted to some simplification. The main aspect of this simplification is the use of four organizing categories, which are essentially analytical touchstones and most certainly do not constitute an exhaustive conceptual framework. The following quote from a history teacher at Flightpath, talking about LMS captures these categories rather neatly.

In that the headmaster is going to be totally preoccupied with accounting it seems, especially in the early years, I mean I think perhaps once some kind of budget plan is in place that it might not be so complex, to use the same budget with adaptations the year after. But then the schools are going into things like more fund raising, advertising themselves, so, in the end the word Headmaster could well disappear and we could have something like managing director of Flightpath School, it might be more of an appropriate sort of title. I don't think that's got very much to do with education, not real education because I think in the end the education happens in the classroom. It needs the guidance, it needs the organization, it needs

the construction, but in the end it also needs of course, above
all, the input in fact of staff to lessons and to obviously what
the school is all about.

(27 February 1990)

Clearly evident in this teacher's speculation about the future are
concerns over the changing relationships between *education*,
management, the *budget* and the *market*. What comes through
strongly in our data is the fact that, in practice, these are
increasingly the central concerns of school life and they appear
time and again in varying combinations.

Figure 6.1   Tensions and dilemmas in the management of school
change

In Figure 6.1 we have represented the *potential* relationships in
the form of an oblong with connected diagonals. However, it is
the precise relationships between these concerns, the way in
which they are seen by practitioners and the outcomes of
struggles between them that actually form the central interest of
the chapter. These relationships can be further rendered as sets of
tensions or a language of dilemmas (Berlak and Berlak 1981,
p.11). To paraphrase the Berlaks, the dilemma language of
management represents the thought and action of senior teachers
(and others) as an ongoing dynamic of behaviour and consciousness within particular institutional contexts. For example:

certainty	– uncertainty
managers	– colleagues
control	– commitment
executive action	– participation
quick responses	– precipitate action
financial planning	– curriculum planning
budget maximization	– educational principles
market image	– educational need
efficiency	– effectiveness

formula funding   – professional judgement
information control   – information dissemination
summative consultation   – formative decision-making
forward planning   – information deficit
innovative responses   – stress and morale
rational planning   – overload and disorder
institutional blame   – system blame
expertise   – alienation
executive headship   – educational leadership
management   – professionalism

It is within these dilemmas that the complexity of what we shall call 'new management' arises. 'New management' is orientated towards and constructed within a discourse of cost, income, efficiency, financial planning, image presentation and enterprise and modelled on the practices of business. But, in the schools, in practice, this 'new management' orientation results in tensions, ambiguities and ambivalences. This is very evident in the language and formalistic contortions represented in some of the quotations included below. These tensions are primarily of two kinds. The first are institutional and emerge from the contradictions between forms of control and forms of integration. That is, between the emphasis on 'top-down' leadership and the clear-cut separation of policy and execution – 'Control is indeed the central concept of all management systems' (Braverman 1974, p. 68) – and the need to maintain the commitment and interest of the non-managerial staff in the development and purposes of the institution. The locus and form of decision-making is important here, as we shall see. Thus, 'new management' stands in an uneasy relationship with existing notions of collegiality and professionalism, although it does provide for the professionalization of the educational manager. The second kind of tensions are those which surround the definition of purpose, and these arise mainly from the constraints, requirements and opportunities created by the provisions of the ERA. For example, as the list above suggests, educational decision-making may be set against budget-led planning, professional judgement against the expediencies of market image and professional autonomy against managerial fiat. Thus, the development of 'new management' is not simply or primarily a structural or administrative change (although new roles and new relationships are created) it is also a profound change in

organizational culture. The complexities of changing management and the management of change are in part defined by these
tensions, but this complexity is exacerbated by the incoherence of
change itself and the fundamental contradictions, or incompati-
bilities embedded in the policy ensemble of the ERA. In other
words, complexity and contradictions are inherent in the tasks
and requirements that schools now face. It may be a mistake to
believe that there are solutions!

The DES claims that the opportunities implicit in devolved
budgets, linked to the motivating force of the market and set
alongside the National Curriculum and national testing, will
have salutory effects upon the management of education in
schools and, thus, result in higher standards. In this respect
management is seen to stand over and above the other categories
as *the* means by which educational improvement will be secured.
This shift in focus is often clearly understood by the senior managers in the schools. As a deputy head at Parkside put it:

> Although we weren't a TVEI school, much to our annoyance,
> we have taken on board many of the things which TVEI in
> terms of industrial relations and the quality of education in the
> classroom. Before that there were the red book papers on
> curriculum development, HMI reports, and we responded to
> many of those. So a great deal has been happening purely on
> the educational front. Then came the Education Reform Act
> and we get things like Open Enrolment, religious education
> and Local Management of Schools, financial management. Not
> just of the day-to-day finances, but the total organization of the
> school and that has really shifted the focus of the management
> team from managing education to managing an educational
> institution. And I think that is a tremendous change.

Our analysis draws upon data gathered between May 1989 and
December 1990 in the four case-study schools and attempts to
'map out' the interplay between the touchstone categories within the four institutional settings; we make particular use of nine
interviews conducted with the deputy with responsibility for
finance and resources at Parkside school. In addition it seeks to
reflect upon the different positions faced by the managers of
change and some of the 'managed'.

The Gap

> It's all down to bucks, kid; everything else is just conversation.
> (Gordon Gekko in Oliver Stone's film *Wall Street*)

In the quotation earlier from the history teacher at Flightpath there is a strong view of the changing role of management and the increasing difference of concerns and functions between the classroom teacher, on the one hand, and the new managers, on the other. Education, management, the budget and the market are seen to be in tension. There is a recognition that each of these 'vocabularies' have their place, but there is a slippage between ends and means in the organization. Or perhaps more accurately the emergence of two rival ends. One, the most important organizational 'reality' as he sees it, is education. The other is the budget. His concern is with the former and, as he sees it, the Head's concern is more and more exclusively with the latter. His suggestion of a change of nomenclature for the headteacher is interesting in this regard and crops up again in several other interviews. What it implies is a rise in the power of the managers via their control of the budget and a consequent erosion of the influence of the classroom teachers in the decision-making process.

This is equally well understood by some members of senior management, but as one of the deputies at Parkside School implies the various initiatives also produce a feeling of being 're-made' by these changes; and sometimes in ways he would not wish.

> Since September I've had the role of finance and resource manager, and I didn't really believe last summer that my job would change so much. But now classroom education is a very low priority, and regrettably so. I regret that I can't give the time to preparing my teaching lessons and so on, I used to. And I'm sure the quality of my teaching has declined. My role here as finance and resources is almost incompatible with teaching in the classroom. But no extra resource in terms of teacher time has been made available to schools, to allow that teaching to take place. So the quality of product for the children has declined.
> (27 November 1989)

Nonetheless he foresees opportunities,

I think ultimately the whole thing is going to be better for the schools. Because much of the inertia which resides in civic centres will be removed. But what we need to get is the people with salaries equivalent to people working in civic centres moved out to schools so schools have the extra support to do the job more effectively. At present I see that LMS is almost going to be a cost-cutting exercise, moving work from the civic centre to the schools but no extra people to do it. And I think that would be an opportunity lost. I think a promotion of the idea that our roles have changed and the development of the staff is a slow and difficult one. They still see, and indeed we're called, deputy head teachers, and the teacher aspect looms largest in the eyes of many of the practising teachers in the school. I think that is something we have to show them, that we are still concerned with teaching and the quality of teaching but of necessity we're taken further away from it. Only the other day someone came into me and said 'what are you doing in here, where have you been all this term?' – and it came home to me then, that this has taken me away from the daily contact which I had with people last year, and I've made an effort to get back out again. But today for example, or this week all my non-teaching, non-contact time is taken up with going to meetings, or meeting people or organizing things, concerned with finance and resources, and not with promoting the grass roots educational programme of the school. And in fact I could very easily spend my entire time involved in finance and resources without being all that directly involved in the education process. That is, I think, regrettable.

(27 November 1989)

There is very strong awareness of the nature of his new role and his separation from classroom-based colleagues. He has ceased to be a deputy head 'teacher' and is now a 'finance and resource manager'. And the senior management team are, as he puts it, no longer managing education but managing an educational institution. Educational concerns are becoming consumed or perhaps subsumed by a new set of broader institutional concerns. Here then again is a version of the tension between education and management as different 'possible worlds'. One of the other deputies:

I don't think that the Education Reform Act, if you asked a general teacher and said, what are the implications of that, I don't know whether they'd be able to respond to that in terms of the management of the school. That's where the major areas of change have been, because the Education Reform Act has dictated that, has dictated the role of deputy head has had to considerably change. Has had to change because of new-found responsibilities. But the teaching staff are unaware, simply because they haven't got the time to plough through the implications of what is imposed upon deputy heads, in terms of managing the school. So their single interpretation of deputy heads is that they distance themselves more and more from real life, by sitting in offices, and working on computers and handling bits of paper. They don't belong to school any more, and it's the hospital analogy thing, you get the managers of the hospital who are non kind of medical and that's what's in danger of happening. So it's a very difficult situation for me. I've always had a policy to work with the staff. I go into the staffroom, I talk to them, I have lunch with them, but that's always created a problem for me because I have to take all the snipes and the jibes. It sounds like I'm feeling sorry for myself, but people will always turn to me. They won't go to the others, they've become more and more unapproachable, because of their roles.

(14 November 1989)

As a curriculum deputy he has a position within the school that requires the sort of contact the other deputies are finding difficult. He acts as a sort of a valve for the frustrations some of the rest of the staff feel over the growing gap between the classroom teachers and the senior management. But this new 'role' provides its own frustrations as he now stands in a dual relation to the staff and to senior management. He 'understands' both parties, he stands between and inhabits their two worlds but he feels unable to secure a permanent reconciliation.

One way of thinking about this is to see it as the emergence, in schools, of what Foucault refers to as a 'heterotopia', that is the coexistence in 'an impossible space' of a 'large number of fragmentary possible worlds'. 'Characters no longer contemplate how they can unravel or unmask a central mystery, but are forced to ask, "Which world is this? What is to be done in it? Which of myselves is to do it"' (Harvey 1989, p.48). The choices or possibilities or confusions with which people are confronted produce tensions within individuals (even a sense, perhaps, of post-modernist schizophrenia) and between individuals as they attempt to resolve these tensions in different ways. As an aside, we would note that in more general terms the same schizophrenic tensions are represented in the ways in which schools present themselves to their 'consumers'. Schools are expected to achieve and represent what Jencks (1984) calls a 'double-coding', (although he is referring to post-modernist architecture). One code speaks of a tradition which is slow-changing, which echoes the familiar aspects of 'good' schooling, reproduces the cliches of what Metz (1989) calls 'real school'. The other represents fast-changing society, new skills and tasks, new technologies and ideologies. The contradictions inherent in these 'codes' make for a heightened sense of tension as well as potentially fracturing the teaching staff. The 'gap' is one manifestation of the way in which some schools have sought to solve their institutional dilemmas. The double bind is that the 'solution' only appears to create further or second order tensions and dilemmas; the 'them' and 'us'!

The dilemmas.

'Sometimes you eat the bear and sometimes the bear eats you'.
(North American Indian Proverb)

It is crucial to realize that these changes are not artefactual or epiphenomenal, they are not transitional but arise from the intentions for change embedded in the ERA. This is evident in the following discussion with one of the Parkside deputies about his future role. Asked whether things would 'settle down' after a transitionary period he replied:

Quality control is going to be essential when you have a surplus of places. A surplus of schools in the local authority within an area chasing pupils, that the competition between them is such that a great deal of time is going to be spent on promoting your initiatives as opposed to delivering the product within the school. It's got to be spent on showing outsiders what you do, much more than educating the children within it and I think that is a shame. I think if we were in the situation where we were all assured of our security, we would still give a high quality service, we wouldn't be distracted by seeing if we can survive. But there's no doubt about it that schools which are successful in the early years of LMS are going to be shot at by other schools, it's the natural thing, schools feel that they have a right to exist and people have got their hearts and minds, entire careers tied up in institutions, which they deeply believe in, and they're not going to see it sink, and they're going to try to show it's better than the other places. And if we offer true opportunity to have different experiences in school, that's one thing, if we try to show that other schools in some way are not as good as us, I think that's detrimental to the cause of education generally. My worry is we shall spend so much time arguing and looking over our shoulders at what other people are doing and what other people are saying about us, that it may neglect what we're actually doing ourselves . . .

(27 November 1989)

What is evident here again is the tension between education and the workings of the market, between 'service' and 'survival'. The deputy head does not see it disappearing and he is very uncomfortable about promoting image over education, but he is also clear that the pressures of competition are likely to increase rather than decrease. Very similar sentiments are expressed by one of the classroom teachers at Flightpath:

I don't know, I really don't know, . . . however the school is marketed. I mean it concerns me a lot and I also have a sort of inbuilt resistance to some of it, as well. I find it very sad that actually schools are spending so much time and energy on, you know, glossy brochures and I know we have to but I also think it's very sad, because actually, to my way of thinking what, the best marketing the school can do is actually, will be the current pupils, what is going on in the school and parents' views on the school.

Interviewer: So do you feel in a sense that the Education Reform Act, in all its glory has actually produced a situation that is very difficult for schools to escape from?

Very much so, and yes, I do think that very strongly, that schools are, have found themselves in a situation that they are not in control of, over LMS and with all those things being together that actually they have got no control over what they're implementing.

(28 February 1990)

What both of these extracts allude to is a shift in the locus of control over schooling from the professional producer to the market forces of consumption, this shift is mediated, as in 'real' markets by financial concerns. Being a 'good' school is no longer enough, schools must now become 'good' businesses. But that shift is not as simple or as unproblematical as it sounds, for what these participants in the shift are indicating is that it also involves a shift in values as well as a change in focus. The values and focus of 'new management' are no longer derived from the 'educational' per se. However, we are not suggesting that the 'new managers' are hostile to the new conditions of schooling, that is certainly not the case. They may express some ambivalence, discomfort and regret but they also see possibilities and opportunities. 'Doing the best for the school' can involve significant rethinking of sources of income and patterns of educational provision.

So it may well be that ultimately we'll get a different form of spending and we'll also be funded more on an industrial basis. Which takes us to another area really which is the income generation. Which we now regard as essential, especially the 9.2 acres we've just been given, and the development of that for recreational purposes. I'm contacting various people to see if we can raise some sponsorship or loans to make that an all-weather surface, which we can then let out and generate income from. But we have to make sure that we are in an area of the market which we can guaranteee income from for many years. That's the sort of area we're into. And also I'm writing to companies, a circular letter, asking if we can interest them in us training their staff in terms of modern languages in preparation for 1992, in terms of basic level IT training. Not necessarily a fee basis for this, but they would provide resources for us in kind and then we would carry out some sort of training facility for them.

(27 November 1989)

In this instance the growing need to generate a 'guaranteed income', in turn generates a whole variety of non-educational activities that can only result in a continuing erosion of his position as an educator. Nevertheless, the 'thrill' of securing funds for the school, the deep sense of protection and caring for an institution that could be threatened continue to force him to 'go down that path'.

> I foresee the situation where we could buy in the sessional tutors, in the same way as adult education does at present, buy in more of those to provide the training, or we could simply extend the contracts of our existing staff to train these people, if they're willing to accept that, and any income we get use that for buying in extra staff into the school, so maybe for example you've got a true need in a school for say two-and-a-half business studies teachers, but you'd employ three-and-a-half the salary of one would come out of the income generated from the training of personnel from industry and so on.
>
> We're just pushing our luck really, to see what we can get but I see no reason to see why somewhere like Dixons or Comet shouldn't provide us with some electrical equipment as well and some sort of advertising even to go with it, you know, telephones or televisions or whatever 'courtesy of Comet'. But in addition to that we could train staff as well. These are just ideas which I'm just trying to flesh out. It's the sort of way I think that some colleagues have been thinking of going. I don't see why schools, especially community schools shouldn't become involved in the same sort of thing. You see we have to make ourselves indispensable as far as the local community is concerned, that's the business community as well as the pupil community.
>
> (Deputy, Parkside, 27 November 1989)

Clearly, there is much here which accords with the version of an educational marketplace which has been advocated by the various neo-liberal visionaries who have flitted in and around No. 10 Downing Street in recent years. And Secretaries of State, Baker, McGregor and Clarke have all talked about the way in which LMS and Open Enrolments would serve to release enormous entrepreneurial energy in schools. Part of the role and spirit of the 'new managers' (in some schools) does offer evidence of such a release. But again matters are not straightforward and neither managers nor classroom teachers seem keen to place the market over education. There is the strong sense of the market as a compelling force, something that cannot be ignored *even if* it distracts and detracts from the job they felt they came into teaching to do.

Nonetheless, there is at least a 'cultural resistance' to the new metaphors of purpose and a defence of traditional roles. Some teachers stress the 'clash of interests' between marketing activities versus educational activities. The Head of Overbury, is very ambivalent about the use of industrial 'vocabularies' to discipline schools.

> I think it's the idea that the school is a factory, and that you have a product, which you're shoving out into the market, and if you don't do it or do it inefficiently, you will therefore lose money. I mean the whole of that idea I find repellent, but it doesn't mean that all of the processes of industry and management should be as alien to schools as they have been for many many years in the past.

While the management techniques of business may hold some attraction the discipline of the market does not. Not suprisingly she proposes a different solution to the change in role and orientation that she faces – the appointment of a financial specialist. Here the staff and she would maintain a primary concern for teaching, for education, the finance and resources manager would provide 'efficient structures'.

> A Bursar at £20,000 a year, and a finance and resource manager, it's at a couple of levels above what we would expect to pay someone in charge of a school, and that person will – I've got the job spec here – that person will actually have some routine tasks, as someone doing the filing, would do, so they are administrating the budget and they are controlling finances. And that includes equipment and the school's and the administration's systems, and all of the non-teaching staff, so they would be making recommendations about the efficient use of resources, they will be looking at not just the servicing end of things – what do we do to get this equipment repaired – but what equipment should we have and who will use what. There would be someone in charge of the cleaning and caretaking who will report to them. They will be in charge of all the staff in the office, and their job will be devising efficient structures, of people and for admin. To make the whole school

run efficiently and effectively, in order to leave teaching staff free to actually get on with teaching. I mean I see it so much as a key appointment.

The question is whether the classification and framing that the Head of Overbury proposes between the roles and authority of teachers and manager can be maintained. (This is a point we return to below.) But this, or some version of it, is clearly an attractive alternative for many Heads. The Head of Parkside sees the answer in having specialist roles for his deputies leaving him to concentrate upon the 'quality of education'.

> But the freedom which LMS gives you to apportion resources and make the decisions, is I think, a very positive and exciting freedom. But what is easy to do is to get bogged down in things like that. I don't particularly want a computer in my room, I don't think my job is about getting involved in that. Making policy decisions, okay, but I think my job is about improving the experience in classrooms, about improving the quality in classrooms. And that's why you need people like Bill, you need people to do it, okay, but you've got to be very careful about you as a Head, getting too bogged down to the detail and the nitty-gritty of it all.
>
> (14 November 1989)

Overall the Head takes a positive view of educational reform. He sees the ERA as having a galvanizing effect and presenting possibilities for real change, although he accepts that a number of aspects of the Act were, so to speak, already firmly on the educational agenda. But in relation to these changes he hopes to preserve a version of leadership which is essentially 'educational' and thus avoid the most pressing aspects of financial management; as we have seen, these are to be taken on by one of the deputies.

> I think this is a very exciting time to be in education. I think that we have a greater chance now of improving the quality of education than I think we ever have had. Yes, a lot of things that the Education Reform Act talks about were already there, like assessment, it was already on, already the idea of meeting criteria of establishing certain attainment targets, yes, that was already there. I think there's a sense of purpose in education now, which probably wasn't there ten years ago. This would

have happened perhaps without the Reform Act as well because things take so long to change in schools and I think that probably it's only in the last five years that schools have really taken on board the implications of a comprehensive system, because for a long time I think schools tried to be philosophical. We have always taken on change, in a half-hearted way, and we always half regret what we've lost. That was true of education because we always half regretted grammar schools and what a lot of people in education tried to do in a sense was to keep the grammar school thing going.

(14 November 1989)

The Senior Deputy at Parkside saw two models of headship beginning to develop in schools:

One would be a Head who is very much an administrator and site manager, who leaves the running of the curriculum to the deputy head and the management team and deals with the people who just run the establishment, and may be an entre-preneur, gets money to enable others to do the job. Or you may well get another scenario where the Head is the curriculum leader, and delegates the rest to a deputy head or bursar or site manager. I don't think you'll build up a head who can do both, I think the job is too big for one person to do.

(5 June 1989)

For the headteachers, part of the problem of responding to initiatives for educational change is retaining control over all the varied aspects of their domain and the activities that take place within it. This places a strong pressure upon Heads and senior managers to 'manage', i.e. to re-create and rebuild, reconstruct and redefine the institutional context and the places of those within it as well as those significant others who stand 'outside'. This involves the development of new roles and relationships and thus a new institutional culture. The interview data from the Heads shows this process in action. Thus they talk of 'creating the right environment', 'avoiding getting too bogged down in the detail and the nitty-gritty of it all', 'leaving staff to get on with the teaching', 'freeing teachers from the burden of LMS' and 'taking the strategic reins'. As Ball (1990c) points out, all this only heigh-tens the belief in 'management' as a panacea for solving the dilemmas and easing the tensions. This also appears to have a gender aspect in the sense that the classical notion of rational-deductive management has strong overtones of 'macho male-ness', as portrayed by McGregor (1967, p.23):

> The good manager is aggressive, competitive, firm, just. He is not feminine; he is not soft or yielding or dependent or intuitive in the womanly sense. The very expression of emotion is viewed as a feminine weakness that would interfere with effective business processes.

Management conducted in this fashion often becomes task orientated and the 'personal' is not expected to interfere in the drive to complete tasks. In addition concern about 'relationships' within senior management teams and between teams and the rest of the school is displaced. When connected to a strong sense of collective responsibility and commitment to the institution this notion of management puts a great deal of pressure upon individuals to deliver, whatever the personal cost.

Our data also shows that many senior managers hold a strong belief in applied rationality, a commitment to the power of logic. That is the view that if only they could get the systems and structures 'right' then everything else will fall into place; complexity will be simplified, contradictions resolved, tensions and conflict virtually eliminated making the institutional context more 'manageable'. These ideas are often expressed in interviews in the duality of certainty/uncertainty, the view that current structures and processes of management are not quite right and do not work – but with the appropriate changes things could be 'got right'. The Senior Deputy at Parkside again provides an example:

> The four deputy heads had informal discussions with the Head, as individuals. And then he came up with four packages, with very loose titles and very loose definitions within them, and we were invited to take them away and look at them. We did that. And the four packages are the finance and resources package, the curriculum initiative package, research and development, and the community package. In the past we've had very much a matrix system, where everybody had some developmental, some curriculum, some pastoral . . . some administrative roles to perform. And on the face of it those will still exist. Everyone will have a variety of activities but it is

much more specialized than it used to be, with someone very much finance and resources, someone very much curriculum. I don't know, I think in the early years of LMS that probably this is the right way to go because the whole range of new activities you're going to have to take on board, is very complex. And someone I think has to oversee the finance and resources, but then you see it goes back to the LEA notion than local management of schools is about finance and resources. And what I think has got to happen is in addition to having these roles for deputies, there's got to be a much more coherent whole-school policy and three, five, eight-year plan of where we want to put the school in a few years' time. If we have that planned and where we want to go then these different people can contribute to it. But if they're contributing just to make the finance and resources efficient, or the curriculum efficient, then it's not really going to work. They've got to work within clearly defined parameters . . . My own goal is finance and resources and that's a big move for me because I was really most qualified in terms of curriculum. But the worry about that is that I shall be seen as a bursar in the school and that's what I don't want.

(2 October 1989)

Corwin (1983, p.214) captures the essence of this belief system very nicely:

'Rationality' results from the integration between means and ends, which is produced by interdependency and firm control by enlightened administrators. As Gouldner (1959) observed, in this model the structure appears to be entirely manipulable and designed solely for purposes of efficiency, and any departures from rationality can be attributed to mistakes, ignorance, or miscalculation. The keys to this model then, are administrative control coupled with expertise and integration among the various components of the organisation.

This would serve as a mission statement for virtually all the senior managers we interviewed. However, our point here is that the drive to gain control of the internal aspects of school life may well be continually thwarted by the external, often uncontrollable, 'disciplines' of the market, balancing the budget, inspections, accountability and the National Curriculum. The schools operate within a 'precarious' rather than a 'domesticated' environment (Corwin 1983, p.234). Taken together with the pace of change these external elements often leave senior management having to take decisions with a minimum of staff involvement and heighten the tension between the staff concern to be self-determining and 'the managers right to manage'!

MANAGING WHAT?

This brings us back to the issue of control over decision-making and the tension between market/budgetary and educational priorities. The 'gap' between 'new managers' and teachers is, as we have argued, not simply a division produced by role specialization. It also represents a division of values and purposes. Many senior teachers we interviewed were attempting to find some kind of resolution to the consequent tensions. Thus a senior teacher at Flightpath sees it as a matter of establishing a balance between the marketing of the school and its income, on the one hand, and making the right choices for individual students on the other. But he is under no illusions that this balance is easy to achieve or maintain.

> You are caught and this is where LMS really raises its ugly head, in terms of true educational things. Each child has a price tag on it, and the sixth formers have the highest price tag. So in pure financial terms one obviously is trying to raise the most amount of money you can. But Flightpath staff have always been conscious of our intake being skewed towards the less able child, and through the years we have developed what has got to be considered one of the best supportive education departments in the LEA. In fact I'd go even further, I'd say we've got to be the best. And in recent years they have not only taken the lower ability children, but also have been aware and have tried to help the more gifted children as well. But of course the less able children tend not to stay on to the sixth form, unless we feel they are really going to benefit from it and we have an excellent record, through our guidance department of ensuring that our children get into employment as well. So you have this conflict of trying to ensure you've got a big sixth form, trying to ensure that you are really doing the best for the individual child, and the introduction of the

disabled children. I don't think that that is sort of a problem for us in terms of whether it was a bad image or not. I think personally it can do nothing but good for us but one has got to recognize the fact that these children do take a lot of extra time. Certainly from just a pure administration point of view, and a commitment from our own staff, on top of the other staff coming in from Mapledene school. One has obviously got to get a balance between the demands of our ordinary child here, and the less gifted child, as opposed to the amount of hours that one puts in onto a relatively small number of children, and we are in the process at the moment of negotiating with the authority, for more financial support, either through the form of better facilities for them, and/or more staffing levels, and that's all in the melting pot at the moment . . .

(23 March 1990)

A whole variety of dilemmas are embedded here as the school's educational 'mission' is made to face up to the 'realities' of the new regime of funding. The key question facing the senior management team is, how far can they go in ignoring the financial realities, in balancing principles against cost. The financial managerial priorities of LMS call into question the appropriateness of effective provision for students with special educational needs. Again two value systems and also two locii of organizational control are adumbrated. Reflecting upon the early days of the School Management Plan the Senior Deputy at Flightpath certainly portrayed the balance as at least being lopsided.

The School Management Plan is really an LMS centred one . . . which has grasped the fact that financial planning cannot be divorced from the development plans of the school, which is not to say we've actually achieved an integrated plan, we haven't. That's one of our problems, that's probably the most major flaw in our document. But it was because the nature of forward planning became clear, the fact that we would be simultaneously reviewing a cycle and planning for a year to three years ahead and that whatever management processes we have already in the school we couldn't really cope, and therefore what we needed was to reconstitute the senior management team, as a broader team, this was our interpretation, to include non-teaching staff.

(16 January 1990)

Here is the uncertainty/certainty principle again. These comments underline our previous point about the link between problem-solving and getting management systems right. The reconstitution of the senior management team being suggested here is one of several competing and sequential restructuring plans which were floated and then abandoned. For example, in direct contrast to the senior deputy's vision of a broader based management team the Headteacher of Flightpath outlined the following model.

> In managerial terms the senior management committee is hopelessly too large, and what you've really got to see is that here are our deputy heads and here is our senior management team, and they have assistants attached to them . . . personal assistants with whom one is undertaking a continuous process of in-service education. I think this matter of line manager accountability is something that's going to be sharpened by LMS.
>
> (6 July 1989)

As so often, as Coopers and Lybrand (1988) and the DES (1988a) urge, new forms of management are directly linked to the implementation of LMS.

Further evidence of the division/gap between management decisions and educational ones *and* the articulation of that division in terms of decisions related to the negotiations over and allocation of monies is to be found in the following comments from the Senior Deputy at Parkside.

> If we're talking in terms of the management team of the school directing changes within the curriculum then really we ought to be working out with departments what is required in terms of money, but also what we think is required in terms of them putting forward a plan and having a coherent strategy for growth, across the departments which is management led. In the past you see, with the administration of funds, I've asked departments to make a fairly detailed submission of what they estimate is their needs for the year, and then discussed it with them and massaged the figures really to enable them to do things. But going for much more of the impersonal formula, and then allowing the departments to make of it what they can, in some ways, unless we're very careful, I think that could

be a dereliction of duty on the part of the management team, to manage the curriculum. And I think the other thing that could arise from that is that departments will say 'oh well they're just passing the buck over to us, they don't really care, why should we care'. But when we were involved in the day-to-day process and discussions with them, they felt at least we were supporting them, even if they were short of money. But I think they may well lose confidence in the system now. In much the same way as the school you know is basically losing confidence in the local authority, 'cos they can't identify historic costs for us, and we think while they've been incompetent in the past, they just dish it out by formula now, they don't really care what's happening, or appear not to care what's happening. The same sort of alienation could be found within the school.

(4 April 1990)

This deputy also sees dangers in these new kind of relationships, in particular an alienation effect arising from the replacement of professional/collegial relations with financial/managerial ones. The use of a formula for allocating monies would be typical of the latter, whereas a professional exchange related to educational needs in terms of historic costs represents the former. Embedded in these dualities and oppositions is yet another one. That is, the tension between effectiveness, as the meeting of needs, and efficiency, as the minimization of costs in relation to output. However, this is a distinction that is often obscured in the political rhetoric about LMS, possible tensions and differences in purpose are thus glossed over. The interplay between cost analysis and measures of performance within the context of LMS also raises a variety of possibilities for the monitoring and control of teachers. From this point of view the LMS package can be seen as being as much disciplinary as it is administrative. The disciplinary scenario is explored in the following extract of an interview with a classroom teacher at Flightpath.

To what extent LMS is going to become an oppressive dark shadow over say how well a teacher teaches examination classes, that could prove to be contentious. The use of incentives for example, to reward so-called good teachers, which is very very difficult to arrive at. It's based on the classes you're teaching anyway, the resources you've got, and various things like that. Staff appraisal of course, could be something that could be used in perhaps a much more insidious way, I think, because yes, under LMS or whatever, it's presumably going to be quite possible, I think it states in the article yesterday that a headteacher who was very well sort of organized with LMS, could begin to say to himself, well look, that lesson is costing me so much today and the history lesson is costing me so much, how cost-effective are they both, and what are the teachers like in both those lessons, and how much am I paying one, compared with the other, and I think that's a possibility that could be quite serious in time to come.

(27 February 1990)

The fear here is that a model crudely linking pay to performance could be the logical conclusion from placing LMS and appraisal together in the institution. Then place this in the market and he is clearly worried about the loss of control for teachers and schools. He goes on:

It is the market forces, which is in fact where I think again education is going to be hijacked, perhaps badly you know. As was said for example, in one of the videos we saw, as a sort of introduction to the National Curriculum, we are not like the marketplace, we can't change, we can't get rid of, what was the sort of phrase, unproductive sort of products, like certain pupils. We have to carry on, and maybe evolve the situation which we could perhaps make our pupils more productive. But how do you do that, well I suppose the variety of ways for the future could be endless, like opting out or with greater selection procedures going on or in fact a kind of selling of the school to the feeder primary schools in a way that would try and get say the primary schools to feed particular kind of pupils into your school. And all these kind of ruses could be brought about, and that in fact makes education much more of a manipulative sort of thing in a way. And yes, there is the marketplace operating very strongly, and yes, teachers are under pressure to produce. In the end of course, what may well become perhaps the whole reason for the exercise, these wonderful glowing exam results, at the end of the exercise, where you are in the pecking order, how your school fares. Because in the end, when the parents in fact of tomorrow or whatever, armed with the National Curriculum, and with various other sorts of government information, are going to ask that question, 'it's all very well your school having this wonderful building and these marvellous computers, but what are your exam results like', and everything becomes very empirical in the end, doesn't it. It's all quantified to how many As and Bs and Cs you've got, and what staff are getting these and what staff are not and therefore of course if they're not, what can be done about it.

(27 February 1989)

These changes are seen as totalizing in nature. Educational effects are reduced to a set of crude outcome measures which represent the school and provide for comparisons between teachers. The interrelation and interpenetration of budgets, governance, management, assessment, curriculum, employment and pay, appraisal and promotion, and collegial relationships all combine to produce what he sees as a nightmare world. However, the institutional responses to these changes are not, as we have been at pains to point out, of a piece, neither are they free-floating or random. They also relate to the micro-markets within which the schools are nested. By micro-markets we refer to the competitive environment within which the schools are set. Thus it is not altogether surprising that Flightpath and Parkside schools, both in Westway authority, are markedly more attentive to market issues than, Overbury and Pankhurst, both in Riverway authority. The Westway secondary schools operate in a highly competitive environment, there is a significant surplus capacity of secondary places in the authority. Nonetheless, institutional cultures do play a part in the moulding and selection of managerial responses to LMS. In the run-up to LMS the Head of Pankhurst was adamant that her school's priorities would remain firmly within the realm of the educational, even though she saw herself operating at a disadvantage in relation to one of the school's major competitors, a girls' independent school.

But I've got to make a stand that standards must not be lowered and if there is a deficit it'll have to be carried forward, and the pressure, believe you me, will be on the local authority, to increase the amount allocated, rather than for me to have to start cutting, 'cos I don't think I'm prepared to do it. It seems to me we operate absolutely on a shoestring. I've got the Highcliffe figures, the independent school, it used to be the

grammar school of this area, but when we went comprehensive it went independent. I think student numbers are
about the same overall, they have a big sixth form, but they
have smaller entry, and are more top heavy, so of course there
would be additional costs, but their budget is £2,382,289, for
the current year. Now that is more than double ours . . .

(28 November 1989)

At the time of this interview the Head was under the impression
that the budget at Pankhurst could be as much as £100,000 in
deficit in the first year of per capita funding. But in some senses
the curriculum-led planning approach is a luxury that Pankhurst
could afford, its unique position as the only girls' school in the
authority, its longstanding reputation for academic achievement
and thus its fairly secure recruitment position made the need to
link the budget to the market relatively less pressing. In some
ways Pankhurst is the least budget-conscious of our four case-
study schools. The 'educational' and the 'financial' seemed to be
strongly bounded off from one another.

I don't think that the middle management know anything
about LMS or care anything about it and I think that they
always wish they had more money. I think they believe I'm
doing my best with the money available. I mean they see the
allocation of funds, that's discussed, and except that they all
want more, nobody ever really challenges, nobody has the
courage to challenge any other department. They never say,
there's too much put into capital and not enough for the departments. Nobody's ever said that, and I don't know whether
it's lack of interest or whether they really think it's as satis-
factory as we're likely to get. I hope it's the latter.

(28 November 1989)

Nonetheless, Pankhurst is not neglectful of the need to attend to
its public image, nor is it unaware of competitive relationships
with other schools.

The Pace

To lose heart is to lose confidence and meaning. For many
teachers and administrators, the rapid pace of change has torn
the heart out of schools. Heart will not be restored by

knowledge; it can only be restored by dancing and healing. But this will require a significant shift in our thinking about how schools can be changed. At the very least we can stop running them by promoting change and reform that weakens the moral fibre of schools, thereby dampening the promise for the future ahead.

(Deal 1990 p.147)

We have tried to give some indication of the complexities, tensions and load created by the management of change and changing management in schools and we have hinted at the impact of the pace of change. It is this latter aspect that we now want to take up in more detail.

There are three sorts of issues that could be dealt with roughly under the heading of pace. One is, straightforwardly, the feeling that there is inadequate preparation and planning time to do what is expected from the ERA. A second, is the degree to which initiatives follow and overlay one another. A third, is the extent to which information, documents and proposals relating to change, from various quarters, are drip-fed, countermanded and changed. Where there is little time, considerable overlap and continual information deficit, management tends to become a haphazard process of intuition, guesswork and ad-hockery, with decisions having to be made without adequate information, then having to be remade in the light of new, sometimes unexpected developments (Fullan 1982, Wallace 1990). It is often the case that the writers of policy texts suffer from the single change perspective and themselves fail to grasp the complex interdependence of school decision-making. Different policy agencies aim discrete policies at the same target institutions with overlapping, short-term time-scales for response and do not co-ordinate among themselves. All of this makes a mockery of the neat and trite prescriptions offered in many of the 'how-to-do-it' management texts written to cash in on the ERA reforms. Wallace (1990, p.13) notes that:

Managing multiple innovations, many of which were externally imposed, appeared to differ in kind from the management of a single innovation in that it was an ongoing, day to day process of juggling with a continually shifting profile of innovations in the context of other work rather than the sequence identified in the literature on single innovations ...

It is clear from the interviews that some fine judgements were required about the timing of decisions. Experience of the National Curriculum and LMS quickly demonstrated that pre-cipitate action was often counter-productive, 'things change', and then change again. The Head of Overbury speaks here as a recently appointed Head:

> It appears to me as though the amount of information that comes in and the amount of things one is required to do grows and grows and grows and grows, and it doesn't just come in in a steady stream, it's actually multiplying. One is required to get parents involved, governors involved. Things you've got to consult with staff about, is also growing and growing and growing. I find the fact that I didn't know how things worked before actually makes life quite difficult, and I sometimes get the sense that I could, almost, at one time have coped. If I tick off the things that are coming in now, which are obviously new things, I often think, if only I'd had some time to get to grips with things, before the LEA had started to move then it really would have been much easier. And I gather from talking to other heads, who've been in post a long time, that that is partly true, that they actually feel that they had the time to become a new headteacher. At the same time people who've been in post a very long time, people who are very resistant to the changes have got perhaps a different kind of difficulty, in that they're having to throw out old ways of thinking, whereas at least I'm not having to remould my way of thinking. What I would appreciate is a time when I could stop and mould a way of thinking, without feeling I needed to alter it because of some-thing I heard on the radio on the way to work, or some new kind of development, which needs to happen because of relationships with governors, which are still at the stage of being forged and new kinds of relationships with PTA which is still at the stage of being forged.
>
> (15 January 1990)

One important aspect of this, as she points out is that many of the changes in management and the management of change relate to new kinds of working relationships, with governors, teachers and parents. The development of these new relationships is not helped by lack of clarity, changes of mind and incomplete docu-mentation on the part of the initiators of change. Structures can be manipulated and restructured infinitely, people cannot. (In particular all of the Heads from the case-study schools were critical of poor handling of the LMS pilot year by their LEA.) The senior deputy at Flightpath gives some indication of the tension between having to make decisions and not having enough information on which to make them properly.

Take the National Curriculum, for example. We knew, probably something like two-and-a-half to three years ago that National Curriculum was coming, but it's a word and a vague notion, and it's what you read in the educational press. Certain changes were already on our timetable, because of what we took to be the direction that National Curriculum was moving us towards. In retrospect I can see that what we were thinking about was a core curriculum, rather than a National Curriculum, but we didn't know that at the time, because we didn't know what National Curriculum was. All we were dealing with were vague notions. So I think this is a good example because you can see that a lot of planning, we're talking about things where meetings went on, where decisions were taken, we're talking about things which were built into our previous plan, but now looking back on it you can see that they were based upon inadequate information. They were good for what they were doing at the time but in the perspective of now! Information is coming through much more strongly of course. But also because we are forced to allocate money, we're forced to allocate staff responsibility, we're forced to give a target date for when something will happen and we're forced to consider what resources and what in-service training. Now you might say that we should have been doing that three years ago, or even last year, but I would say that until schools feel that they have a degree of certainty about what funds they have control over, in what kind of cycle of expenditure, they won't do that, they just won't do it. I mean we have to establish a totally artificial situation similar to LMS, before you do it or you'd have to be a martinet and run the school more along business lines.

(16 January 1990)

Planning, forms of control and lack of certainty interplay here. Part of this complex process of judgement about when and whether to act in relation to specific changes also relates to the

feeling that several senior staff articulated that they needed at
times to protect their teachers from the full impact of a succession
of changes or to put it another way they were aware that the
energies and tolerance of their staffs were not infinite. The Senior
Deputy at Flightpath takes this up. (Note again the priority, as
constraint, given to financial planning.)

We've started from the point of view that finance is something
that you can work out, as a sort of definite constraint to all your
planning. We've talked about it vaguely from time to time, but
just as important, is teacher time. And there is a tendency to
say, look this is where the buck stops finance-wise, if you
haven't got the money you can't do it, but not to apply the
same sort of stringency when you're talking about staff time
resources. We've only got a limited amount of staff time
resources, we can't handle this, this is where it stops – bang.
We talk about it in vague terms, that we're possibly overloading people, but we don't actually itemize it all out and say
we are overloading people, this is it, cut it out, it's not going to
happen. It's as if people will accept the financial argument. If
there's no money for it you can't do it, they'll say fine. But you
know, they'll always say yes, you can squeeze a little bit more
time out of this or wouldn't it be a shame to lose this initiative.
There's all kinds of ways of phrasing it, so that the poor old
teacher at the centre of it all, ends up shouldering endless
additional tasks.

(16 January 1990)

Thus innovation overload is not just an institutional problem, it is
a problem for innovators, the people. Innovation overload and
information deficit combine to produce high levels of stress and
declining morale. The Head at Overbury drew attention to
another crucial point that is easy to miss in the heat and noise of
the ERA. That is, there is more to school and the running of
schools than the ERA. As a Head she has an agenda of concerns
that extend to other issues, an agenda that is being brought into
direct focus by the demands of LMS.

There are some things which are not ideal about LMS, and they
are bringing to bear pressures on schools which one would have
hoped not to have had, and one of the things I think is the whole
thing of marketing, which, if we are not careful, is going to
become too sharp. Like the school that was giving a 10 per cent

reduction on showers. It seems to me that that is a kind of excess which one wants to avoid. But LMS is not just to deal with that, it's easy to quote these things and say well therefore LMS is ridiculous. LMS highlights the really rather old-fashioned, rather inefficient, and in some cases, a bit slovenly way in which many schools might have been run. I mean we should have in schools what LMS is helping us to achieve. We should have very clear procedures for the disposal of money. We should have everyone in school with a proper job specification, for whom they are responsible and who is responsible for them. We should have a school which is running efficiently with proper procedures for an administration, disposal of money, and all these sorts of things.

(15 January 1990)

(Again the language here is interesting in relation to the point about 'getting things right' and proper procedures for administration. In all of the schools this seemed to be a promised land that everyone believed in but no one seemed to quite reach.) It is also important to make the point that planning requires particular skills and resources. It depends on having appropriate information (schools need to know things that they never needed to know before), it also depends upon the assumption of some degree of stability, but it is not easy even without the uncertainties of a turbulent environment. There is an apparently irresolvable contradiction between the need for forward planning – a need which is both practical and emotional -- and the year-on-year marketing, recruitment and budget allocation established by the system of LMS and formula funding. The senior deputy at Flightpath talked about this:

It's forward planning that makes the difference. It's remarkable in the past what forward planning spans there are, cycles to your curriculum planning and all the rest of it which are set and established. But even there by January you would have made, and this is historically what is happening, you will have made certain about what you're going to get in terms of staffing, and so on and so forth. And schools have been locked into these very small planning cycles. You'd never have started considering what you might have done in 12 months' time, because of the level of uncertainty about the next few months. I'll give you another example. This year they've introduced a 5 per cent carry over of credit or debit on capitation, but we couldn't make a decision about our final spending for this financial year because we didn't receive an audit of our accounts for the previous financial year which had ended in April '89, by November of '89 and by November of '89 you're in the position of having to spend. And we didn't know, even by that time, whether we'd under-spent or over-spent by 5 per cent or whatever, had no knowledge of it at all. I had to get on to the Assistant Director of Education and harry him for some weeks before I actually got the information, that we were under-spent by £500. Now that gives you some indication of how schools have operated in the past, with the minimal financial information. And therefore you can understand, it wasn't just a decision that schools came to at some stage, that they wouldn't plan ahead. I think all schools would dearly have loved to have planned ahead, but the degree of their certainty about the future was so low, that they haven't ever been in the position to do that. Having said that, of course, there are these broad planning strokes that run through everything that schools do. It's just that you can't actually get from these broad strokes to precise detail, so no one ever has made that connnection, and actually having to make that connection hurts, it's quite a painful process because not only are other people at fault in the authority and so on, one realizes oneself that we are at fault, in not being clear enough and precise enough about all kinds of things in the school which until you've sat down to do that exercise you don't fully appreciate.

(15 January 1990)

Here again, in a different form, is the uncertainty/certainty duality. The need for planning certainties are confounded by the ever present uncertainties of recruitment and the budget. Again, though much of the 'failure of certainty' that results is 'felt' (painfully) to be a result of the inadequacies of planning procedures within the school, this may actually be a 'displacement of blame', away from the system itself where it may more properly belong.

So often it would seem the pace of change means that the most important (or interesting) is forced out by the need to attend to the most immediate, the most pressing. For the would-be 'new manager' this is a further source of frustration.

All four of us, including Miriam, feel we're increasingly bound down by administration, rather than by management and policy making. And we had high hopes of big changes five or six months ago. The weight of admin. is bearing down upon us. I think one of the things that has been hindered a bit is creativity . . . I have to pay so much attention to detail and sorting things out in the short term, that being creative, and long-term planning, is difficult.

(Parkside deputy, 26 March 1990)

The crucial element in all of this, as Wallace (1990) notes, is the retention or creation of 'room for manoeuvre'. That is being able to reassert some degree of control over the processes of change. But given the multiple determinations and the interrelations within which schools now operate, any sense of being 'in control' of events is fragile to say the least. We would want to underline the role of ad-hockery and muddling through. Here the senior deputy from Flightpath talks through one period of decision-making which linked LMS closely to constraints upon class size.

Gosh, looking back to that time, you remember how at sea you felt with the whole thing. You go back to that context of inadequate financial information. You've got major decisions to make about staffing and so on at Easter time and we came back from the Easter holiday deciding that there was such a gap of understanding between what we were grappling with and what heads of department didn't know anything very much about, that we'd have to do something quite special, in order to improve the consultation. The consultation having not worked the way we set it up, we had to immediately set up something that would work, and the idea was over the holiday itself, to haul in the director of studies and the head of special needs for the whole day, bring your lunch and we'll sit there with the figures, and the Head and I went through the whole of the LMS staffing, the whole of the way LMS worked with two people, because they were asking such pertinent questions about it, that we couldn't answer them in the kind of time that you normally have available. So all of us gave up a whole day to understand it better, and as a result of that we decided to have an emergency meeting on the Friday, after school, with all heads of department in which they crystalized their understanding of where special needs existed, in order that we could explain to them what we were doing with set sizes and setting blocks, and so on and so forth. Because although you had general ideas about it, you now had to get this hardened up. Now that was extrememly valuable, and it was done very much in an emergency sort of form but it came out of very real questions about. Why can't we have this, why can't we have that?

(28 November 1990)

Again here the shortness of timescales is evident and problems involved in getting internal processes right vitiate the response to outside events; the result is 'an emergency sort of form'. We should also note perhaps that he is talking here about explaining, justifying decisions that 'we' made, the point of the exercise was not to debate or consider alternatives but to understand that there is no alternative.

For better or worse, in most schools the Head remains the 'critical reality definer'. The Head is the primary mediator and interpreter of change and thus has significant influence over the institutional pace of change. Wallace (1990, p.9) reports from his study that: 'The headteachers, in association with staff and governors, acted as "gatekeepers" for the adoption and adaption of innovations, whether internally initiated, or externally resourced or imposed.' And 'The beliefs and values of heads concerned not only the innovation itself but also their judgements about whether or when to implement it so as to maximise what they perceived to be the school's advantage or to minimise negative effects' (p.10). But Heads may make errors of judgement or at least find themselves blamed for aspects of the process of change which are beyond their control. In the talking about the disorganization and complexity of change we are trying to indicate how some wrong footedness seems almost inevitable. Given the emphasis upon the executive role of the Head, he or she is most likely to be the object of blame when things go awry. The response of staff to their Head's management of change attend to both matters of substance and matters of style. One of the junior deputies at Parkside, is critical of his headteacher's style and pace of the management of change.

When I thought about it, that's how I would enter a school as a headteacher. I'd want to listen to people. Because if you make changes immediately, it kind of undermines what's happened. James hasn't done that, he's made a lot of changes. He's changed the management structure. He's changed our roles within it. It has created some animosity between Bill and Alex and myself. Although we've never talked about it, it's evident. His style is totally opposite to the last Head. It's determined, at the least . . . in terms of getting his way. And it's very very fast, and I know that Bill and Alex and I have all sat back and said, this is all happening too quickly for us. Because we've had to make decisions about the curriculum and we've been pushed to make decisions right now, decisions that we've felt needn't be made right now. Changes have taken place, it's difficult to describe, but it's just very very fast. And it's different to the way it was. I'm all in favour of change, when it's change for the better. But I think it's fair to say that the staff are now standing back and saying, 'Now what's happening here'. One minute this is happening, the next minute it's changed. And the other criticism is that he has preconceived ideas. Alex, who's wonderful at drawing up little anecdotes and analogies said that this headteacher is doing the 400 metre hurdles, rather than a middle distance run, and I have some sympathy with him, but it's a big change in management style.

(14 November 1989)

It may be again that some displacement of blame is involved here. As 'gatekeeper' the Head is being blamed for the pressures of change that he cannot altogether contain. There is little room for manoeuvre. The dynamics of internal change are again seen to vitiate responses to external change. As in the earlier extract from Flightpath, it would seem that coping responses which adapt internal structures to cope with one set of changes at one point in time turn out to produce difficulties for coping at a later point in time. Change is being coped with from an unstable, even crumbling base. Here is the problem of institutional change in changing institutions, of changing management and the management of change.

Change always threatens a culture. People form strong attachments to heroes, legends, the rituals of daily life, the hoopla of extravaganza and ceremonies – all the symbols and settings of the workplace. Change strips down these relationships and leaves employees confused, insecure and often angry.

(Deal and Kennedy 1982, pp.157–8)

Decisions and making decisions

> Providence gave men the power of speech so that they may better disguise their thoughts.
>
> (Talleyrand)

In this section we want to say something about management roles, changing management and the management of change in relation to decision-making in a slightly broader sense. Significantly, for the most part, when senior managers in the case study schools talked about decision-making they tended to talk about themselves making decisions; although in a least one of the schools the role of governors was beginning to impinge significantly upon the relative autonomy of the Head and deputies. But it is also recognized that decisions have in some ways to be justified to the teaching staff, especially those decisions which affect their work directly. Heads and deputies were variously aware of the need to maintain institutional commitment and integration in order to retain staff, encourage work effort and maintain or improve student performance. Yet the nature of this justification or legitimation of decisions and thus the relationship of teaching staff to the decision-making process was distinctly unclear. The words employed were often vague and meanings shifted. All of this related of course to the gaps and tensions outlined above. Thus, for instance, one of the deputies from Parkside seems to want to hold both ends of the chain when he talks (see below) both about the staff 'accepting the expertise' of the management team and 'gaining their support', but also 'the principle of participation' which, in the past, had 'led to a good group feeling'. These views of the decision-making process do not seem entirely compatible but rest perhaps on the meaning of the term 'participation'.

I think we've got a responsibility to draw up plans to put them forward for serious consideration, unless there are overwhelming reasons why they shouldn't go ahead. If it can be proved conclusively that we've made a cock up then things should be thrown out of court, but by and large staff have got to accept that we've got a deal of expertise to offer and we've thought carefully about it, and this is the way we think the school should go and we're asking for their support to carry it through. I think if we go to them openly, and the staff have confidence in us that we can carry things through. I think if we let it go too long and don't publicize very much at all then they'll begin to lose confidence in us and it'll be quite difficult to get their support. 'Cos the change in style, it's not just the change in style for the management team, there's a change in style for the entire school and one of the things I used to hold was working parties on various topics based on the principle of participation, anybody could attend. We always made sure we had somebody from every department and so on were there, but anybody could attend. And that led to a good group feeling amongst staff, and if we suddenly throw that out then some of the staff are going to feel devalued, so I think it's important to go for consultation quite soon and we will!

(27 November 1989)

For the Head at Parkside the 'problem' of participation again emerged in terms of 'getting things done', two irreconcilable agendas. His solution involves a kind of compromise wherein decisions are made and then tested. This might be seen as a kind of 'summative' involvement rather than a 'formative' one. Both of the major issues introduced so far are embedded here. First the new executive roles of the senior staff reinforce the separation of policy from execution. Second, the pressures produced by the pace of change militate against cross-institutional involvement in decision-making. And yet the speaker still recognizes the need to maintain commitment. The solution is openness and consultation at some later point in time. Parkside seem perched on the brink between an old collegial style of organizational decision-making and a new managerial style and a very different set of relationships.

I think if we spend a long time about arguing where we're going or what we should be doing, then ultimately that ends in feelings of frustration. I think what people want is for somebody to know where he's going or where the school's going, they want to be told, they want to be informed, they want to be consulted, they want to have a voice in the way this is put together, but I don't particularly think that they want to be very much involved in the decisions about where we're heading, where we're going. I don't mean that to sound authoritarian, obviously not, 'cos one of the things that I'm doing with the curriculum is that I'm talking to heads of departments about it, and seeing what they think about it, and if there is a lot of hostility I would think about something else. You have to put out feelers, don't you, you have to modify and everything, but I think at the end of six months we're going to come out with something which I, which we, will have a lot of confidence in.

(14 November 1989)

Also, perhaps rightly, the Head doubts the 'will to participate' of his staff. The Head at Overbury articulates a similar kind of ambivalence about the role of staff, and reiterates the deputy at Parkside's point about the privilege of specialist knowledge. This further underlines the 'gap' between management and teacher, policy and execution. Here consultation is an additive rather than a formative process, a matter of elaboration rather than fundamental decisions; a recognition of 'new realities'. The flood of documentation aimed at the headteacher effectively reinforces her executive position and disqualifies teachers from participation.

Where do you draw the line, do you start with a blank piece of paper. What do we need to do in the school? Do you start there, or do you start by giving people some suggestions, or do you start with a fully fledged thing, saying well this is what I think, do you want to add to it? I think it's likely that what will happen is that we identify several areas, and at the moment I have on paper those areas which only which I think are important, many of those areas have come from what I know to be the main concerns of staff at the moment. And I would intend discussing that initially with deputies, and then bringing the paper to the next senior management meeting that we've got, for their suggestions as to how we proceed. Which will either be to put that paper to a staff meeting, or to the school advisory committee – which are heads of department and heads of year. And what I would envisage asking for is any additions, and what people feel the priorities are. I would be asking for people's ideas, which would then be amalgamated into it, I would not be setting up the priorities on that management plan, totally because 20 staff had felt that and two staff had felt that. It is important, very much, to hear what staff think are priorities, but there are sometimes priorities coming from outside which staff possibly can't see, and why should they be able to unless they sit down for a million years and go through all the things . . . And I also find that if you're not careful, are you actually patronising, I'd like to listen to you but basically, you know, it's only me that knows. I'm saying, I'm a manager, it's only me that knows what's going on up there.

(15 January 1990)

It is perhaps a little unfair to simply say that these Heads want to have their cake and to eat it too. They do want to make their own decisions but they also need to have staff support. The senior deputy at Flightpath explains some of the dilemmas he and his colleagues face with regard to consultation with staff, particularly when developing the new management plan, as they are expected to do by the DES. The School Management Plan had initially been written over a period of several months by the senior management team. But when released to staff it was not well received and a series of discussion meetings were set up with the possibility, a rather unclear possibility, that the plan would be revised. But even then the revision process is an executive, managerial one rather than a participative one. In a sense the medium is the message, this is a school *management* plan.

It could be that we did it wrongly and I think that is certainly arguable, that we took very much a top-down approach. But I would still argue that it is immensely difficult to have the levels of participation in your initial planning. Because with the best will in the world teachers are only going to take on board so much. They don't really want to be loaded down, with a vast amount of planning, resourcing issues of the whole school. [Research, Chapman 1990, suggests he is right.] Let's just look at where we are with this particular plan we are now reviewing it, and I've been talking with deputies about reviewing it. I haven't been talking with anybody else, no wider audience, just with the deputies, because I still feel we have not got the capability for other people to get involved very much in the review, except insofar as they are named people in the management plan that we produced last year. So obviously if they're named people, and they received the plan. They would be expecting to be asked questions about their role in the plan.

(28 November 1990)

Looking at the extracts together there are some interesting contradictions in the evidence. The status and purpose of consultation
remain unclear *and clearly vary*, the senior management in these
schools choose when to consult and when not to. There is clearly
a question of staff interest and expertise in relation to certain
issues, but also the constant pressure to make decisions quickly.
The instrumental, social and micro-political purposes of consultation are confused and overlain. The pressures to manage
change produced by the ERA emphasize the role of 'new management'. The expertise *and* the concerns of staff and management are increasingly divergent. *And* there is nothing in the form
or spirit of the legislation which gives value or credence to staff
participation in school management or governance, quite the
opposite.

CONCLUSION

The source or the moment of specific decisions within institutions
is often elusive, decisions often appear to emerge rather than get
made in any simple sense. This makes the art and act of management itself both elusive and even mystical. What is important
perhaps is the changing institutional culture within which
decision-making and management are set. Overall, the Heads
and deputies we have interviewed and quoted convey a sense of
frustration, doubt and concern about the management of change.
The changes they confront as a result of ERA and other recent
policies are overlain, interrelated and often contradictory. As we
have seen a lack of clarity and inadequate information combine to
produce an air of desperation with regard to decision-making
and forward planning. The complexity of change is exponential.
There is always a potential for chaos. The solution is seen to be
management, and more management.

There is a degree to which it is the rational patina of management discourse that actually provides the sense of a future state of
good order, the long-term 'cure' against the threat of chaos. Thus in
a context which *is* increasingly complex, ambiguous and disordered
it may be that the language of management and rationality perform
a symbolic function. To contemplate that this might be the wrong
language, that it misrepresents the true state of things would be to
contemplate the unacceptable. Estler (1988) argues exactly this.
Hence the tenets of technical–rational management:

Provide a 'kind of legitimation' by giving the appearance of rationality to processes necessarily surrounded by ambiguity, it lends meaning to the lives of participants who live in a world valuing rationality; and it provides a sense of order to participants in an environment that is often disorderly.

(Duignan 1990, p.334)

As we have seen, information as a basis for decision-making is regarded by school managers as critical. Perversely though, there is a tension between too much information and not enough, between overload and deficit. There are crucial issues related to information flow and the control of information. There is a contradiction between dissemination and communication, in order to facilitate and legitimate change, and the retention and manipulation of information to provide control. The gap between policy and execution looms large. Information reinforces expertise.

It is information on which you are going to base decisions, which is crucial to local management, and the ability to vary inputs and parameters and make decisions, informed decisions. So the whole question of information, reliable information, is crucial. I mean if we cannot have that then we're back to a pen and paper exercise, which is slow and may well lead to inaccurate or inappropriate decisions being made . . .

(Deputy, Parkside, 5 October 1989)

The rigours of LMS and 'the budget', and the pressure to change established social relations, which clearly cannot be escaped from, privilege and legitimate management and rational epistemology as the one, the only possible form of organizational decision-making and control. But what is clear throughout the data presented here is that the simplicities of rational management continually fail to match up to the complexities of change. Note that Malen, *et al.* (1990, p.289) conclude, from an exhaustive review of the American literature on school-based management that: 'There is little evidence that SBM alters influence relationships, renews school organisations or develops the qualitities of academically effective schools'. Perhaps we can leave the very last word to the classroom teacher at Flightpath, quoted at the start of the chapter:

We went through I think a period at one stage, late sixties, early seventies, certainly in the seventies, where I think perhaps we did lose sight of the examinations, there tended to be a period when the exams weren't really that important, education was much more a developmental, rounded approach to the human being and so on, and maybe we went a bit too far that way. I suppose that's part of the product of course of the sixties and so-called respectability of the individual and the so-called egalitarian society that was supposed to emerge after the post-industrial era, whatever you like to call it, which didn't materialize at all. And I think that that is in fact what is, is sad now. We're into a situation now where I think we definitely are not in control, I don't feel in control. I may feel consulted, but the consultations are more or less about what's been discussed and decided, as opposed to what in fact we are going to do. And I think as well that, even the style of perhaps even heads of departments is becoming like that too, they're finding their room for manoeuvre is not that great either. So I'm not blaming them so much, they're being told to implement things therefore they're coming over as being quite, not perhaps dictatorial, that's too harsh a phrase, but, but perhaps as being determinedly persuasive, that's what's going to happen. And no doubt they're looking over their shoulder, because they're being told, look, you are the one who is accountable, so get these things done. And that's it, the directive is, is taking shape rather like you know we have time, people think . . .

(27 February 1990)

References and further reading

Adler, M., Petch, A. and Tweedie, J. (1989) *Parental Choice and Education Policy*, Edinburgh, Edinburgh University Press.

Ainley, P. (1990) *Training Turns to Enterprise: Vocational Education in the Marketplace*, London, Tufnell Press.

Alder, M. and Raab, G. (1988) 'Exit, choice and loyalty: the impact of parental choice on admission to school in Edinburgh and Dundee', *Journal of Education Policy*, 3, (2), 1988.

Alford, R. and Friedland, R. (1988) *Powers of Theory: Capitalism, the State, and Democracy*, Cambridge, Cambridge University Press.

Apple, M.W. (1983) 'Work, class and teaching', in S. Walker and L. Barton (eds), *Gender, Class and Education*, Lewes, Falmer Press.

Association for Science Education, The British Association and The Royal Society (1991) *Only a Teacher? An enquiry into Science Teacher Provision*, London, Association for Science Education, The British Association and The Royal Society.

Atkinson, P. (1985) *Language, Structure and Reproduction*, London, Methuen.

Ball, S.J. (1987) *The Micro-politics of the School*, London, Methuen.

Ball, S.J. (1990a) *Politics and Policy-Making in Education: Explorations in Policy Sociology*. London, Routledge.

Ball, S.J. (1990b) 'Education, inequality and school reform: values in crisis!', inaugural lecture, King's College, London.

Ball, S.J. (1990c) 'Management as moral technology', in S.J. Ball, (ed.) *Foucault and Education*, London, Routledge.

Ball, S.J. and Bowe, R. (1990) 'The micropolitics of radical change: budgets, management and control in British schools, paper delivered to the American Educational Research Association Conference, Boston, 1990.

Barry, N. (1987) *The New Right*, Beckenham, Croom Helm.

Bash, L. and Coulby, D. (1989) *The Education Reform Act: Competition and Control*, London, Cassell.

Berlak, A. and Berlak, H. (1981) *The Dilemmas of Schooling*, London, Methuen.

Bernstein, B. (1975) *Class, Codes and Control*, Vol. 3, *Towards a Theory of Educational Transmissions*, London, Routledge Kegan & Paul.

Bernstein, B. (1986) 'On pedagogic discourse' in J.G. Richardson (ed.) *Handbook of Theory and Research for the Sociology of Education*, New York, Greenwood.

Blase, J. (ed.) (1991) *The Political Life of Schools*, Los Angeles, Sage.

Bolam R. (1982) *Strategies for School Improvement*, report for OECD, Bristol, University of Bristol School of Education.

Bondi, L. (1989) 'Selecting schools for closure: theory and practice in rational planning', *Journal of Education Policy*, Vol. 4, No. 2, pp.86–102.

Bourdieu, P. and Passeron, J.-C. (1977) *Reproduction in Education, Society and Culture*, London, Sage.

Bowe, R. and Ball, S.J. (1990) 'Managing change in the educational market', *The Journal of the Centre for the Study of Comprehensive Schools*, Vol. 2, No. 2, Spring 1990.

Bowe, R. and Ball, S.J. (forthcoming) 'Subject to change? Subject Departments and the "implementation" of National Curriculum Policy: an overview of the issues', *Journal of Curriculum Studies*.

Bowe, R. and Whitty, G. (1989) 'The reopening of the GCSE "Settlement": recent developments in the politics of school examinations', *British Journal of the Sociology of Education*, Vol. 10, No. 4.

Bowles, G. (1989) 'Marketing and promotion', in B. Fidler, and G. Bowles, (eds) *Effective Local Management of Schools*, London, Longman.

Braverman, H. (1974) *Labor and Monopoly Capitalism*, New York, Monthly Review Press.

Brown, P. (1990) 'The 'third wave': education and the ideology of parentocracy', *British Journal of the Sociology of Education*, Vol. 11, No. 1, pp.65–85.

Caldwell, B.J. and Spinks, J.M. (1988) *The Self-Managing School*, Lewes, Falmer Press.

CCCS (Centre for Contemporary Cultural Studies) (1981) *Unpopular Education*, London, Hutchinson.

Chapman, J. (ed.) (1990) *School-Based Decision-Making and Management*, Lewes, Falmer Press.

Codd, J. (1988) 'The construction and deconstruction of educational policy documents', *Journal of Education Policy*, Vol. 3, No. 5 pp.235–48.

Coopers and Lybrand (1988) *The Local Management of Schools: A report to the DES*, London, Coopers and Lybrand.

Corwin, R.G. (1983) *The Entrepreneurial Bureaucracy*, London, JAI Press.

CPS (Centre for Policy Studies) (1988) *The Correct Core*, London, Centre for Policy Studies.

Cultural Studies, Birmingham (1991) *Education Limited*, London, Hutchinson.

Dahl, R. (1970) *Who Governs?*, New Haven, Yale University Press.

Dale, R. (1989) *The State and Education Policy*, Milton Keynes, Open University Press.

Dale R., Bowe, R., Harris, D., Loveys, M., Moore, R., Shilling, C., Sykes, P., Trevitt, J. and Vasecchi, V. (1990) *The TVEI Story: Policy, Practice and the Preparation of the Workforce*, Milton Keynes, Open University Press.

Deal, T. (1990) 'Healing our Schools: Restoring the Heart', in A. Lieberman (ed.) *Schools as Collaborative Cultures*, Lewes, Falmer Press.

Deal, T. and Kennedy, A. (1982) *Corporate Cultures*, Reading, MA, Addison-Wesley.

DES (Department of Education and Science) (1987) *The National Curriculum 5–16: A Consultation Document*, London, DES.

——(1981), *Education Act*, London, HMSO.

——(1988a), *Education Reform Act*, London, HMSO.

——(1989a), *National Curriculum: From Policy to Practice*, (Sections 4.3 and 9) London, HMSO.

——(1989b), *The Local Management of Schools* London, HMSO.

Doyle, W. and Ponder, G. (1977–78) 'The practicality ethic in teacher decision-making', *Interchange*, Vol. 8, pp.1–12.

Duignan, P. (1990) 'School-based decision-making and management: retrospect and prospect', in Chapman, J. (ed.), *School-based decision-making and Management*, Lewes, Falmer Press.

Edwards, T. and Whitty, G. (1990) 'Urban education after the Reform Act', BERA conference paper, Roehampton Institute of Higher Education.

Elster, J. and Hylland, A. (1986) *The Foundations of Social Choice Theory*, Cambridge, Cambridge University Press.

Estler, S. (1988) 'Decision Making', in N. Boynan (ed.) *Handbook of Research on Education Administration*, New York, Longman.

Eveland, J.D., Rogers, E.M. and Klepper, C. (1977) 'The innovation process in public organizations', Nostrand Science Foundation report, mimeo.

Fidler, B. (1989) 'Strategic management in schools', in B. Fidler and G. Bowles (eds) *Effective Local Management of Schools*, London, Longman.

Freeman, A. and Gray, H. (1989), *Organizing Special Educational Needs*, London, Paul Chapman.

Friedman, M. (1980) *Free to Choose*, Harmondsworth, League.

Fullan, M. (1982) *The Meaning of Educational Change*, New York, Teachers College Press.

Fullan, M. (1991) *The New Meaning of Educational Change*, London, Cassell.

Galloway, D., (1990), 'Was the GERBIL a Marxist mole?', in P. Evans, and V. Varma, (eds) *Special Education: Past, Present and Future*, Lewes, Falmer Press.

Gillborn, D. (1991) 'Crisis management: the effects of national reforms on a progressive school', research paper, Qualitative and Quantitative Studies in Education, University of Sheffield.

Gleeson, D. (1989) *The Paradox of Training: Making Progress out of Crisis*, Milton Keynes, Open University Press.

Goodchild, S. and Holly, P. (1989) *Management for Change: The Garth Hill Experience*, Lewes, Falmer Press.

Gouldner, A. (1959) 'Organizational analysis', in R. Merton, L. Bloom, and L. Cottrell, (eds) *Sociology Today*, New York, Basic Books.

Halpin, D. (1990) 'The sociology of education and the National Curriculum', *British Journal of the Sociology of Education*, Vol. 11, No. 1.

Harvey, D. (1989) *The Condition of Postmodernity*, Oxford, Basil Blackwell.

Hawkes, T. (1977) *Structuralism and Semiotics*, London, Methuen.

Hayek, F. (1976) *Law, Legislation and Liberty*, Vol. 2, *Rules and Order*,

London, Routledge and Kegan Paul.

Hellawell, D. (1990) 'Some effects of the national dispute on the relationships between headteachers and school staffs in primary schools', *British Journal of the Sociology of Education*, Vol. 11, No. 4, pp.397–410.

Heward, C. and Lloyd-Smith, M. (1990) 'Assessing the impact of legislation on special education policy – a historical analysis', *Journal of Education Policy*, Vol. 5, No. 1 Jan–Mar 1990.

IPPR (Institute of Public Policy Research) (1991) *Markets, Politics and Education*, Education and Training Papers No. 3, London, Institute of Public Policy Research.

Jencks, C. (1984) *The Language of Post-modern Architecture*, London, Routledge.

Jonathan, R. (1990) State education service or prisoner's dilemma: the "hidden hand" as a source of education policy', *Educational Philosophy and Theory*, Vol. 22, No. 1.

Jones, K. (1979) *Right Turn*, London, Radius.

Keat, R. (1991) 'Introduction: Starship Britain or universal enterprise', in R. Keat and N. Abercrombie N. (eds) *Enterprise Culture*, London, Routledge.

Keat, R. and Abercrombie N. (1991) *Enterprise Culture*, London, Routledge.

Keep, E. (1990) "Do borrowed clothes fit?" Some question marks concerning the importation of private sector management and market models into secondary education', Industrial Relations Research Unit, University of Warwick, mimeo.

Kelly, J. (1969) *Organizational Behavior*, New York, Irwin-Dorsey.

Kingman Report (1988) *Report of the Committee of Inquiry into the Teaching of English Language*, London, HMSO.

Knight, C. (1990) *The Making of Tory Education Policy in Post-War Britain*, Lewes, Falmer Press.

Knight, F. (1976) *The Ethics of Competition and Other Essays*, Chicago, Chicago University Press.

Knip, H. and Van der Vegt, R. (1991) 'Differentiated responses to a central renewal policy: school management of implementation, *Journal of Education Policy*, Vol. 6, No. 2, pp.123–32.

Kogan, M. (1975) *Educational Policy-Making*, London, Allen & Unwin.

Lawton, D. (1984) *The Tightening Grip: Growth of Central Control of the School Curriculum*, Bedford Way Papers 21, London, Heinemann Educational.

Le Grand, J. (1990) *Quasi-Markets and Social Policy*, Bristol, School for Advanced Urban Studies.

MacBeth, A., Strachan, D., and Macaulay, C. (1986) *Parental Choice of School*, University of Glasgow, Department of Education.

McCulloch, G. (1986) 'Policy, politics and education: the Technical and Vocational Education Initiative', *Journal of Education Policy*, Vol. 1, No. 1, pp.35–52.

McKenzie, R.B. (1987) *The Fairness of Markets*, Lexington, Lexington Books.

Maclure, S. (1989) *Education Re-formed*, second edition, London, Hodder & Stoughton.

Malen, B., Ogawa, R. and Kranz, J. (1990) 'A review of literature on school based management', in W. Clune and J. Witte (eds) *Choice and Control in American Education*, Vol. 2, Lewes, Falmer Press.

Massey, D. (1984) *Spatial Divisions of Labour: Social Structures and the Geography of Production*, London, Macmillan.

Metz, M. (1989) 'Real school: a universal drama mid disparate circumstances, *Journal of Education Policy*, Vol. 4, No. 5, pp.75–92.

Meyer, W. (1986) 'Beyond choice', in I. Kirzner, (ed.) *Subjectivism, Intelligibility and Economic Understanding*, London, Macmillan.

Moore, J. and Morrison, N., (1988), *Someone Else's Problem*, Lewes, Falmer Press.

NAHT (National Association of Head Teachers) (1990) 'The Marketing of Schools', NAHT Council memorandum, Haywards Heath, National Association of Head Teachers Publications Department.

NCC (National Curriculum Council), (1989) *A Curriculum for All: Special Educational Needs in the National Curriculum*, Curriculum Guidance 2, York, National Curriculum Council.

——(1990) *The Whole Curriculum*, Curriculum Guidance 3, York, National Curriculum Council.

Offe, C. (1985) (ed. John Keane) *Disorganized Capitalism: Contemporary Transformations of Work and Politics*, Cambridge, Polity.

Peters, T.J. and Waterman, Jnr. R.H. (1982) *In Search of Excellence*, New York, Warner Books.

Pound, L. (1990), 'A review of "A curriculum for all: special educational needs in the National Curriculum (Curriculum Guidance 2)"' *Curriculum Journal*, Vol. 1, No. 1, May 1990.

Ramasut, A. (1989) *Whole School Approaches to Special Needs*, Lewes, Falmer Press.

Reekie, W.D. (1984) *Markets, Entrepreneurs and Liberty*, Brighton, Wheatsheaf.

Riseborough, G. (1981) 'Teachers' careers and comprehensive schooling: an empirical study', *Sociology*, 15(3) pp.352–81.

Rizvi, F. and Kemmis, S. (1987) *Dilemmas of Reform*, Geelong, Deakin Institute for Studies in Education.

Russell, P. (1990) 'The Education Reform Act – the implications for Special Educational Needs', in M. Flude, and M. Hammer, (eds), *The Education Reform Act 1988*, Lewes, Falmer Press.

Saunders, M. (1985) *Emerging Issues for TVEI Implementation*, second edition, Lancaster, University of Lancaster.

Sen, A. (1982) *Choice, Welfare and Management*, Oxford, Basil Blackwell.

Shilling, C. (1986) 'Implementing the contract – the Technical and Educational Vocational Initiative', *British Journal of Sociology of Education*, Vol. 7, No. 4, pp.397–414.

Shilling, C. (1988) 'Thatcherism and education: the dialectics of political control' paper given to the International Sociology of Education Conference, Westhill College, Birmingham.

Stillman, A. and Maychell, K. (1986) *Choosing Schools: parents, LEAs and the 1980 Education Act*, Windsor, NFER/Nelson.

Strauss, A. (1987) *Qualitative Analysis for Social Scientists*, New York, Cambridge University Press.

TES (Times Educational Supplement) (1989) 'Another crusade that must be won', 26 May.

——(1990) 'Mrs Thatcher signals "U-turn" on curriculum' and 'What the Prime Minister said', 20 April.

——(1991) 'Tories urge change in law: High Court backs "open door" LEA admissions', 31 May, p.2.

Torrance, H. (1985) 'Current prospects for school based examining', *Educational Review*, 37.

Troman, G. (1989) 'Testing tensions: the politics of educational assessment', *British Educational Research Journal*, Vol. 15, No. 3, pp. 279–98.

Von Mises, L. (1976) 'Human action', in A. Steed, B. Andrew and C. McNeil (eds) *The Ultimate Foundations of Social Science*, Princeton, NS Nostrand.

Wallace, M. (1988) 'Innovation for all: management development in small primary schools', *Education Management and Administration*, Vol. 16, No. 1, pp.15–24.

——(1990) *Coping with Multiple Innovations in Schools*, School of Education, University of Bristol.

Warnock, Report (1978) *Special Educational Needs: Report of the Committee of Inquiry into the Education of Handicapped Children and Young People*, London, HMSO.

West, G. (1983) 'Phenomenon and form in interactionist and neo-Marxist qualitative educational research', in L. Barton, and S. Walker (eds) *Social Crisis and Educational Research*, London, Croom Helm.

Wexler, P. (1982) 'Structure, text and subject: a critical sociology of school knowledge', in M. Apple, (ed.) *Cultural and Economic Reproduction in Education*, London, Routledge and Keegan Paul.

Whitty, G. (1989) 'The New Right and the National Curriculum: state control or market forces', *Journal of Education Policy*, Vol. 4, No. 4, pp.329–42.

Willis, P. (1977) *Learning to Labour*, Aldershot, Gower.

Index